Jesus' Life in Dying

Jesus' Life in Dying

*Friedrich Schleiermacher's Pre-Easter Reflections
to the Community of the Redeemer*

Friedrich Schleiermacher

TRANSLATED WITH AN INTRODUCTION BY
Iain G. Nicol
AND
Allen G. Jorgenson

FOREWORD BY
Terrence N. Tice

CASCADE *Books* • Eugene, Oregon

JESUS' LIFE IN DYING
Friedrich Schleiermacher's Pre-Easter Reflections
to the Community of the Redeemer

Copyright © 2020 Allen G. Jorgenson. All rights reserved. Except for brief quotations in critical publications or reviews, no part of this book may be reproduced in any manner without prior written permission from the publisher. Write: Permissions, Wipf and Stock Publishers, 199 W. 8th Ave., Suite 3, Eugene, OR 97401.

Cascade Books
An Imprint of Wipf and Stock Publishers
199 W. 8th Ave., Suite 3
Eugene, OR 97401

www.wipfandstock.com

PAPERBACK ISBN: 978-1-7252-5400-8
HARDCOVER ISBN: 978-1-7252-5401-5
EBOOK ISBN: 978-1-7252-5402-2

Cataloguing-in-Publication data:

Names: Schleiermacher, Friedrich, 1768–1834, author. | Nichol, Iain G., editor and translator. | Jorgenson, editor and translator. | Tice, Terrence N., 1931–, foreword.

Title: Jesus' life in dying : Friedrich Schleiermacher's pre-Easter reflections to the Community of the Redeemer / Friedrich Schleiermacher ; edited and translated by Iain G. Nicol and Allen G. Jorgenson ; foreword by Terrence N. Tice.

Description: Eugene, OR: Cascade Books, 2020. | Includes bibliographical references and indexes.

Identifiers: ISBN 978-1-7252-5400-8 (paperback). | ISBN 978-1-7252-5401-5 (hardcover). | ISBN 978-1-7252-5402-2 (ebook).

Subjects: LCSH: Schleiermacher, Friedrich, 1768–1834—Criticism, interpretation, etc. | Theology. | Sermons, German—Translations into English.

Classification: BV4282 S3513 2020 (print). | BV4282 (ebook).

Scripture quotations are from New Revised Standard Version Bible, copyright © 1989 National Council of the Churches of Christ in the United States of America. Used by permission. All rights reserved worldwide.

Manufactured in the U.S.A.   10/20/20

To Our Students
whose curiosity has been our sustenance

Contents

Foreword | Terence N. Tice | ix

Jesus' Life in Dying: An Introduction
| Iain G. Nicol and Allen G. Jorgenson | 1

1. On the First Sunday of Lent (Luke 24:25–26) | 26
2. The Disposition in Which Christ Faced His Suffering (John 14:30–31) | 40
3. On the Fourth Sunday of Lent (John 16:32) | 53
4. On the Disposition of the Redeemer in His Final Hours (Matthew 27:46) | 63
5. Passion Sermon (John 19:28–29) | 81
6. The Last Look on Life (John 19:30a) | 95
7. Christ's Last Words to His Heavenly Father (Luke 23:46) | 108
8. The Death of the Redeemer as the End of All Sacrifice (Hebrews 10:8–12) | 118
9. A Consideration of the Circumstances that Accompanied the Final Moments of the Redeemer (Luke 23:44–49) | 133

Bibliography | 143
Subject Index | 145
Name Index | 149
Scripture Index | 151

Foreword

Friedrich Schleiermacher's reputation as a timely, articulate pastor-preacher and as a solidly gospel-oriented, progressive theologian, continually broadened in each period of his life as a candidate for ministry in 1790 through to his death in 1834, and then to the present day. In fact, his Christian worldview still serves well to define much that is markedly "modern" today. Nowhere is this claim more clearly evident than in his sermons. Such sermonic sharing with his "devout friends" both presages and carefully displays his famous critically carved exegesis of the New Testament.

The present collection of sermons on Jesus' redemptive work at his very death comes from a period during which Schleiermacher had reached a peak as a follower of Jesus. At that time, he was gathering his oft taught, most noted works on Christian faith and life. The translators of this volume are well known as open-hearted contributors to current theological conversation. Iain Nicol and Allen Jorgenson, respectively a late-career Reformed scholar and a midcareer Lutheran scholar, are both ecumenically minded and active in Canada and so echo their admired great predecessor from Berlin. Moreover, each has already offered significant translation-interpretations of sermons and essays from among multiple pieces by this outstanding "father of modern theology." Nowhere is his vast *oeuvre* more convincing and inspiring than in this set of sermons bent on explaining Jesus' death, theories about which have traditionally been identified as central to Christianity, and yet are hugely contested amid long-standing, banefully contrasting Christian beliefs.

Fortunately, I can refer here to the latest among critically based, systematic studies of biblical and early patristic literature about Jesus' death:

FOREWORD

Mexico's David A. Brondos's fat, two-volume, thoroughgoing, four-decade investigation titled *Jesus' Death in New Testament Thought* (Comunidad Teologica de Mexico, 2018), with its attention to the New Testament and early church fathers through to Athanasius. Brondos's convincing, authoritative survey leads to a "radical departure" from traditional atonement theories, as did Schleiermacher's sermons and doctrinal treatments. This departure is detailed in documents from the late teens of the nineteenth century, after he had cofounded the University of Berlin in 1810 and had fostered creation and growth of its much-lauded theology faculty until and after his own death in mid-February 1834. The present collection of sermons is an instantiation of his working through this crucial theological issue in a new key. Edwina Lawler and I are looking forward to finishing a closely tied follow-up volume, translating key Easter through Pentecost sermons, which consider the question, "What happened after Jesus' death?"

As readers of this translated work by Nicol and Jorgenson will eventually observe, Schleiermacher's brilliant sermons about Jesus' death are set within the context of Jesus' entire redemptive life and work, not magically located in one final event, even while including it. This point has been noted by Brondos too, although he was not acquainted with Schleiermacher's quite similar replacement of a disputatious array of traditional atonement theories, as was recently averred to me through an interlocutor. So, how can this be? Read on, and find out! Particular details drawn from Paul, Gospel writers and other New Testament writers will reveal the amazing, if scientifically quite believable, similarity of findings.

A final note: Iain G. Nicol, a longtime beautiful, most honorable friend, also a mentor and comrade to his younger cotranslator, Allen Jorgenson, who has become a friend and theological colleague during my own later years, has died after completion of the work. Allen has taken up the finishing tasks most admirably. Iain G., as the elder Scotsman always insisted, should accompany the first name, will also have contributed several translated sermons to the above-mentioned volume by Edwina Lawler and me, to which I adverted above. It is only fitting that, as always, he brought to his life here a deep-going understanding of Christian faith, which he practiced openly and faithfully to the end.

Terrence N. Tice

Denver, December 2018
and August 2019

Jesus' Life in Dying

An Introduction

The Preaching Theologian

The preaching life of Schleiermacher, like those of many theologians, is an underexamined and underappreciated part of his theological contribution. This is unfortunate in that working through sacred texts in sacred contexts provides theologians with the opportunity to assay their thought in the crucible of a community at prayer. Sermons remain a tried and tested way of doing theology in the church and serve as a rich source for those exploring a theologian's deepest convictions.

Schleiermacher was a renowned preacher. Dawn DeVries, in a comparative study of his preaching alongside that of Calvin, notes his appeal to the "poetic, rhetorical and descriptively didactic" in order to illumine, move, and teach his hearers.[1] Terrence Tice comments that his doctrinal decisions echo his sermons, and so we are commended to attend to this important genre in the life of this theological giant.[2] He generally preached extemporaneously, and then rendered his oral work into handwritten form, and thereafter had them printed. He published seven collections of sermons between 1801 and 1833, the result of some forty years of filling a pulpit every Sunday.[3] Scholars have access to a good number of this work in that ten volumes of *Sämmtliche Werke* are sermons, and of these, some 185

---

1. DeVries, *Jesus Christ in the Preaching*, 51.
2. Tice, *Schleiermacher* (Fortress), 33n8.
3. Redeker, *Schleiermacher*, 200–201.

sermons are extant on the Synoptic Gospels and 129 on John.[4] Fourteen volumes (plus an Index) of the *Predigten* section of the *Kritische Gesamtausgabe* is dedicated to sermons.[5]

It would be a mistake to explore the content of his sermons without attending to their form, in the more original sense of this word as *forma* or *eidos* of a thing. Just as, according to Aquinas, the soul is the form of the body, the body of the sermon is formed by that which animates it. But we might first ask what the sermon is for Schleiermacher.

Dawn DeVries helpfully identifies incarnation as the "primary metaphor" for proclamation.[6] Indeed, Mary Streufert names Schleiermacher's understanding of the sermon as incarnational insofar as Christ is truly embodied in the community gathered around the preached word.[7] The theme of *Christus praesens* is thoroughly grounded in Luther's theology and is picked up by Schleiermacher in his understanding of preaching.[8] Redeker notes that "the preacher turns to the church as the community of Jesus Christ, which continually lives in communion with the Redeemer."[9] The community, then, is the instantiation of the very reality of the body of Christ, which is the content of the sermon: sermons seek to communicate Christ to those who embody Christ's God-consciousness. The sermon, then, is formed for and by the community as the bearer of Christ's God-consciousness, a point of central importance as we consider both Schleiermacher's theology of the passion as evidenced in this collection of nine sermons. Here we encounter Christ in community. Readers are invited to rid themselves of an image of a preacher who hands over divine tidbits to spiritually starving beggars. The preacher and the hearer together meet Christ in one another. Sermons are not about the mere passing along of information but are means that convey the very encounter of the living Christ

---

4. DeVries, *Jesus Christ in the Preaching*, 71. See also Kelsey, *Schleiermacher's Preaching*; and Sockness, "The Forgotten Moralist." The nine sermons in this series are translated from Schleiermacher, *Sämmtliche Werke*. Citations from this source will hereafter include the abbreviation SW.

5. Schleiermacher, *Kritische Gesamtausgabe III: Predigten*. This source will hereafter be abbreviated as KGA.

6. DeVries, *Jesus Christ in the Preaching*, 48.

7. Streufert, "Reclaiming Schleiermacher for Twenty-First Century Atonement Theory," 98–120. See also Kelsey, *Thinking about Christ with Schleiermacher*.

8. See Jorgenson, "Martin Luther on Preaching Christ Present," 42–55. See also DeVries, *Jesus Christ in the Preaching*, 9, 10.

9. Redeker, *Schleiermacher*, 206.

in the dynamic dialogue that the sermon occasions.[10] It is this image that mandates readers of these sermons to imagine real people behind Schleiermacher's recurring references to "my beloved" and "dear friends." These phrases are not niceties, but references those in whom Schleiermacher is able to discern the Redeemer, who makes present the faith that is passed on. This allows Schleiermacher's "centrality of living Christian community with the Redeemer within his congregation"[11] to become something of a *cantus firmus* in his theology of preaching and in his preaching of theology.[12] We turn now to consider who this Christ is who is met in the sermon and Christ's repletive wonder of filling the word with his presence.

Christ and Community

The message that Schleiermacher consistently communicates both in his sermons and in his related doctrinal pieces is that preaching is the principal means whereby the God-consciousness is communicated in community. In contradiction to many facile interpretations of Schleiermacher's thought, the focus is on the community rather than the individual introspective consciousness as the locus of salvation. Such an insight unsettles the common mistake of asserting that Schleiermacher is thinking utterly about the individual. Consider the following:

> We have communion with God only in a community of life with the Redeemer. Within this community of life, the Redeemer's

---

10. Streufert's affirmation that the source of faith is Christ present is well taken ("Reclaiming," 102). One is also reminded of Bonhoeffer's image of Christ as the "Between." Such images allow theology to take Christ seriously without falling victim to the attending danger of Christolotry, wherein the Son supplants God, whom Paul commends as all in all (1 Cor 15:28).

11. Redeker, *Schleiermacher*, 208.

12. And so, the famous distinction between Reformation and Roman Catholic Christianity as found in §24 of *Christian Faith* ("Protestantism tends to make the individual's relationship to the church dependent on that person's relationship to Christ. Conversely, however, Catholicism tends to make the individual's relationship to Christ dependent on the church" [Schleiermacher, *Christian Faith*, 153]) needs to be understood in the context that Protestantism aims at "a distinctive formation of Christian *community*" (Schleiermacher, *Christian Faith*, 153 [italics added]). Hereafter, *Christian Faith* will be abbreviated as CF. References to *Christian Faith* will be made using the paragraph and subsection numbers, allowing readers to readily reference the German text and/or other translations. Direct quotations will include the page number from the 2016 translation in brackets.

> absolutely sinless perfection and blessedness manifests a free activity proceeding directly from himself, but the need for redemption within the recipient of grace manifests a free receptivity in the process of taking up the Redeemer's activity into oneself.[13]

"Community" here, and elsewhere, can no longer be thought of solely from the perspective of the individual in communion with the Redeemer, although this too obtains. Community always presumes the congregation as well. Salvation is about "kindling a collective life"[14] precisely because the congregation is the means by which the God-consciousness of Jesus is communicated after the event of the cross.[15] The human nature that is first completed with the appearance of Christ is now communal in nature.[16] And so, Mary Streufert is able to assert that "Schleiermacher helps us to claim Jesus' christicism—his divinity—while at the same time relocating redemption from his death to the ongoing power of Christ found in the preaching of the Word in the Christian community."[17] The Redeemer's reconciling activity is to take up "people of faith into the community of his unclouded blessedness."[18] It is not surprising, then, that Schleiermacher sees justification as an action that is operative via a singular decree for all humankind rather than via isolated divine decrees working on individuals per se.[19]

This is an important starting point as we consider Schleiermacher's reformulation of atonement and its attendant motif of universalism, his theology of creation, and his estimation of the role of Scripture in the life of the faithful. All of these need to be read with attention to his commitment to see the community as the locus and the means whereby the God-consciousness is shared.

---

13. §91 (CF, 559).

14. Tice, *Schleiermacher* (Fortress), 31n5.

15. "We are conscious of all approximations to the condition of blessedness that are present in the Christian life as being grounded in a new divinely wrought collective life. This new collective life works against the collective life of sin and the lack of blessedness that has developed within it." §87 (CF, 544).

16. §89 (CF, 553).

17. Streufert, "Reclaiming," 99.

18. See KGA I.13.2 §101: "nimmt die Gläubigen auf in die Gemeinschaft seiner ungetrübten Seligkeit" (112).

19. §109.3. See also Schleiermacher, *On the Doctrine of Election*.

AN INTRODUCTION

Christ, the Cross, and Atonement

The long-standing question of how exactly it is that the life, death, and resurrection of Jesus effect the salvation, or redemption, of those broken in their relationship with God was no less pressing for Schleiermacher than for his theological sources. He shows little interest in classical atonement theories. Neither does the image of Jesus as the inspiring example, long thought to be the motif he bequeathed to early modern theology, dominate his Christology.[20] But this does not leave Schleiermacher without interest in responding to this inescapable theme of atonement.

What first needs to be addressed in wrestling through Schleiermacher's treatment of atonement is what it is that needs to be rectified, or made right, in expressing the nature of this event of the Redeemer. Schleiermacher famously identifies the human religious experience as one of feeling rather than thinking or doing.[21] This feeling is variously experienced in piety, but religious feeling can be distinguished from other feelings in that it comes with a consciousness of the self as absolutely dependent on God (CF §4), which is equated to being in relationship with God. Of course, absolute dependence in itself is not the condition of piety since everyone is in precisely that condition, nor is feeling of absolute dependence this piety, but consciousness of this feeling (*bewusst sind*, §4) is what is demonstrative of piety. This condition of consciousness—necessary for being in relationship with God—is the subject matter of redemption. This God-consciousness is effected by the Redeemer in community insofar as he communicates his God-consciousness to believers, made conscious of this living in utter awareness of absolute dependence. This communication first happened to those living in relationship with Jesus of Nazareth as he preached and thereby communicated this God-consciousness to his disciples.[22] This was the task of the Redeemer right up to his death when we hear his final sermon composed of his last seven words.[23] This message at the cross was entrusted to the very

---

20. See Streufert, "Reclaiming," 100, 101.

21. *Gefühl* is translated as "feeling" in §3 (KGA 1.13.1).

22. DeVries, *Jesus Christ in the Preaching*, 62: "Just as Christ's incarnation was the beginning of the regeneration of the entire human race, so the erection of a permanent place for the preaching of the gospel among a people is the beginning of that people's regeneration."

23. Hirsch, *Schleiermachers Christusglaube*, 82, notes Schleiermacher's precritical reading of these texts that allows a harmonization of the gospels, although he underscores that elsewhere he engages texts in critical modalities. See n50 below.

small community consisting of the beloved disciple and his mother. From there the message spread, and communication in community came to be the means by which this God-consciousness was, and is, spread imperfectly but persistently through time and place.

Of equal importance in this regard is the notion of the single decree.[24] As in creation, so in God's election, the paradox of the one and all—is there one act by which God intends the divine telos, or many acts?—is resolved in the recognition that this distinction is a function of our brokenness.[25] This singularity does not obliterate the possibility, and perhaps the necessity, of some sort of oscillation in the give and take, the ebb and flow of God's singular decree.[26] But always, this singularity is finally and fully described as efficacious for salvation. Attending this singular decree is a strong conviction that those who are not saved are not *yet* saved, and so stages of humanity are assumed as God accomplishes the divine will.[27] These stages allow for the possibility that a kind of "impression" of blessedness exists in those not yet blessed.[28] Atonement, for Schleiermacher, is about the ever-widening circle of the influence of God-consciousness across humanity, spread especially through the preached word in community. By the power of this God-consciousness, the faithful are able to live out their consciousness of the feeling of being absolutely dependent to the end that human brokenness is repaired and liberation ensues.

This image of atonement replaces language of sacrifice and motifs of payment, and "wounds theology" as well.[29] Schleiermacher avoids an image of the cross wherein Jesus wills to suffer in and for suffering itself. Apart from lack of attention to the historical conditions of the same, such a focus would make self-torture necessary and suffering an example.[30] Self-preservation is a duty, and so commended to believers.[31] Christ suffers, not out of a masochistic animus toward the self, but as a result of historically located compassion.[32]

---

24. See Schleiermacher, *On the Doctrine of Election*, 54–55. See also Tice, *Schleiermacher* (Fortress), 37n47.

25. Schleiermacher, *On Election*, 55.

26. Tice, *Schleiermacher* (Fortress), 42.

27. Schleiermacher, *On Election*, 77–78.

28. §101.4.

29. §104.1.

30. §104.4.

31. §104.4.

32. §104.4.

This particular way of attending to the cross, as a consequence of compassion in context rather than as a price paid to an angry God, ran and runs against many harsh pictures of God. Moreover, Emanuel Hirsch notes that in the theology of Schleiermacher, the image of sinners' *Angst* in the face of a wrathful God is "a basic intrinsic falsehood."[33] Neither the incarnation nor the cross is about appeasing an angry God.

Hirsch notes that the history of the tradition is often read as if there are two sorts of doctrines of atonement: one in which the turning point is to be understood as the incarnation and another in which it is the cross that instantiates this. He also notes that Schleiermacher underscored how the two accompany one another, as one might well expect of a theologian whose sensibilities are informed by the motif of the singular decree.[34] It is for this reason that Schleiermacher can accentuate the importance of the fact that disciples believed without any suspicion of the forthcoming resurrection.[35]

In sum, Schleiermacher's treatment of the cross in relationship to motifs of atonement demonstrates that the cross is not about an abstract payment to a vengeful God, nor about our being rescued from the powers of some evil that might thwart the will of God. This is not to gainsay suffering in the life of the Redeemer, and by extension, the life of the community instantiating the Redeemer's activity, nor the individual participating in this life:

> Christ's suffering is *vicarious*, to be sure, and it so with respect to both of the components of his life just mentioned [Eds.—Christ's active and passive obedience]. This is so, for he fully bore compassion regarding sin, even toward those who had not themselves yet felt a lack of blessedness through their consciousness of sin. However, the evil that he suffered was vicarious in that general sense in which one in which human evil is not present is also not supposed to suffer, but if that person does nonetheless receive evil, that same person is thus struck by it in the place of those in whom human evil is present. Yet in no way does this vicarious suffering make satisfaction. It does not do this in the first case, because those who have not yet felt a lack of blessedness still have to get to that point before they can be taken up into community by him. It does not do this in the second case, because it does not exclude further suffering of the same sort. Rather, all those who are taken

---

33. Hirsch, *Schleiermachers Christusglaube*, 89: "eine einfache innere Unwahrheit."
34. Hirsch, *Schleiermachers Christusglaube*, 90, 91.
35. §99.1.

up into community of life with Christ share in his suffering until such time as sin has been totally vanquished in the human race, satisfactorily accomplished through suffering.[36]

Christ's suffering is truly about com-passion in the sense of suffering with, but in two directions: Christ *suffers with* us to the end that we *suffer with* Christ in the context of the community that is the condition for the possibility of our redemption. Since the heart of his doctrine of salvation is about our participation in him in the community that is composed of persons of faith, this suffering continues until such time as sin is eradicated from humankind and God-consciousness reigns to the end that we, like the One in whom we participate, wholly live on the basis of this. In short, our union with Christ, achieved in the community that proclaims this, enables our relationship with God.[37] It is imperative to underline that this suffering is not something taken upon oneself in a macabre fashion as an act of piety, since such an image might impel believers to imagine a vision of suffering that does violence to grace.[38]

The Cross, Creation, and History

Hirsch, in his study of Schleiermacher's passion sermons, discusses how his treatment of the rending of the curtain in Luke 23:45 underscores this as a symbol of Jesus' turning to the world.[39] The cross, then, is not about a denial of the world, and the history that tells the story of it, but an affirmation of the same. Indeed, Hirsch continues: "The observation that unlike others this was no normal eclipse of the sun but rather that it was something extraordinary is linked to the idea borrowed from the Romantic philosophy of nature, namely, that in certain circumstances wonders of the spirit and wonders of nature accompany one another."[40] Hirsch's attention to Schleiermacher's formation in the Romantic tradition

---

36. §104.4. (CF, 664).
37. §104.3.
38. §104.4.
39. Hirsch, *Schleiermachers Christusglaube*, 81.
40. Hirsch, *Schleiermachers Christusglaube*, 81. "Die Bemerkung, daß es sich um keine der regelmäßigen Sonnenfinsternisse, sondern um etwas Außergewöhnliches gehandelt habe, verbindet sich mit dem aus der romantischen Naturphilosophie entliehenen Gedanken, daß Wunder des Geistes und Wunder Nature unter Umständen einander begleiten."

is important, and although Schleiermacher moves beyond this tradition in significant ways, this emphasis on the revelatory power of the created order remains important throughout his work. Redeker, too, notes this: the doctrines of creation and Christology are bound together.[41] Readers will see this with special clarity in Schleiermacher's treatment of Luke 23:45 concerning the tearing of the curtain of the temple in two. He also makes much of the congruence of the realms of nature, and of the Spirit and grace in this treatment of the doctrine of election.[42] In sum, if there is one eternal decree, this decree has to do with all of reality as a whole. Hence, Jesus' consummation of human nature[43] involves a consummation of all of nature since being human cannot be construed in abstraction from being in all its guises. Hirsch is attentive to this confluence when he comments on Schleiermacher's treatment of Jesus' promise to the robber, "Truly I tell you, today, you will be with me in paradise" (Luke 23:43).

> The "today," as Jesus understands it, is the elevating presence of the eternal and the divine in that which is earthly and transitory, transcending all that is past, all that is determined by the present moment and all circumstances of times to come. "Paradise" is a pictorial expression of the blissful inward experience of the divine love of the Father in hearts, minds and souls. For those who receive this true and eternal love of the Father as the encompassing ground of their lives in this true and eternal today, death and life in the earthly and temporal sense are nothing. They have become simulacra, exposed as such and divested of their own demands by what is higher.[44]

The eternal does not only radically qualify the temporal, but it also transfigures the earthly as God's divine decree takes root in the work of the Redeemer. For Schleiermacher, the cross is the end of the old form

---

41. Redeker, *Schleiermacher*, 206.
42. See the ninth sermon below, 133 ff.
43. §104.4.
44. Hirsch, *Schleiermachers Christusglaube*, 84. "Das »Heute«, welches Jesus meint, ist die über alles vergangene, augenblicksbestimmte und künftige Zeitleben sich erhebende Gegenwart des Ewigen und Göttlichen im Irdischen und Vergänglichen, und das Paradies ist ein bildlicher Ausdruck für das beseligende innere Erfahren der göttlichen Vaterliebe in Herz und Gemüt. Wer in diesem wahren ewigen Heute diese wahre ewige Liebe des Vaters als ihn umfangenden Grund seines Lebens empfängt, dem sind Tod und Leben im irdisch-zeitlichen Sinne ein Nichts, ein vom Höhrerene durchleuchteter und seines eigenen Rechts entkleidetere Schein geworden."

of *Menschsein* and the beginning of a new form.⁴⁵ Our participation in this eternal life, all the same, is experienced in an anticipatory fashion in nature.⁴⁶ Insofar as this is the case, our interest in history cannot wane, and Hirsch notes how Schleiermacher's sermons constitute a search after history.⁴⁷ He notes as well how over the years Schleiermacher's image of Christ as Redeemer and the historical picture as procured from the gospels draw closer together.⁴⁸ Finally, Hirsch asserts: "The discussion here is not about the singular, nor about the method of argumentation but rather about how the essential portrait of Jesus, his preaching, and his history are generative."⁴⁹ The *Christusbild* is sketched in order to generate new life in the context of the community. In the estimation of Hirsch this is the recurring commitment of Schleiermacher's work in sermons and beyond: to bring to view that picture of Jesus whose message grants hearers freedom in their experience of liberation.⁵⁰

45. Hirsch, *Schleiermachers Christusglaube*, 92.

46. Hirsch, *Schleiermachers Christusglaube*, 94.

47. Hirsch, *Schleiermachers Christusglaube*,103: "The analysis of the Easter and Ascension sermons as well as those of the Passion has demonstrated that it was with the most rigorous commitment to truth that in his sermons he also strove to hold to the principles of historical-critical research in establishing the historical reality of Jesus of Nazareth." ("Die Analyse sowohl der Oster- und Himmelfahrtspredigt wie der Kreuzespredigt Schleiermachers hat gezeigt, daß er sich mit härtester Wahrhaftigkeit auch in seinen Predigten an das zu halten gesucht hat, was ihm die nach den Regeln wissenschaftlicher Erkenntnis festgestellet geschichtliche Wirklichkeit Jesu von Nazareth gewesen ist.")

48. Hirsch, *Schleiermachers Christusglaube*, 103-4: "But since that time he worked year after year to relate ever more closely the certainty of the heart and mind of Christ as their Redeemer with the historical reality of the Gospels to each other and to check the connections between them." ("Seitdem aber hat er Jahr um Jahr daran gearbeitet, die Gewißheit eines Gemüts von Christus als seinem Erlöser und die geschichtliche Wirklichkeit der Evangelien eng und immer enger aufeinander zu beziehen und aneinander zu kontrolleiern.")

49. Hirsch, *Schleiermachers Christusglaube*, 106: "Nicht das einzelne und nicht die Methode der Beweisführung steht zur Erörterung, sondern da sich hier wie dort erzeugende wesentliche Gesamtbild von Jesus, seinem Wort und seiner Geschichte."

50. Hirsch, *Schleiermachers Christusglaube*, 108: "As our historical-critical-philological method makes possible the knowledge of Jesus' Word and history for us, it will nevertheless fumble in the dark until by the means of its critical freedom and impartiality, it learns to portray anew a historically authentic picture of Jesus as the One who brings the gospel, now with our new hard-won possibilities of unbiased and factual expression freed from every obligation to the tradition." ("Die Erkenntnis von Jesu Wort und Geschichte, wie unsere modern historisch-philologische Wissenschaft sie uns ermöglicht, wird so lange im dunkeln tappen, bis sie es lernt, im Medium ihrer kritischen Freiheit

In sum, as we look at Schleiermacher's sermons on the passion narrative, we will do well to remember that his theology endeavors to do justice to Jesus' life, and it refuses to imagine the gospels as passion narratives with extended introductions. This does not mean that these narratives—with deep resonance in the lives of the faithful—are irrelevant but that they are read by Schleiermacher through the lens of the life of Jesus in these sermons. The history of the tradition, in large part, has done the reverse.

Schleiermacher and Scripture

Schleiermacher's astute work in hermeneutics has clearly been of profound importance for the Western intellectual tradition in fields of theology and philosophy, and beyond. His work in this area was fed in large part, yet not solely, by his work in and commitment to biblical texts. Sermons gave him opportunity to put his hermeneutic insights to homiletical utility. In preparation for what follows, a few comments on his use of Scripture in general and in the nine sermons, are appropriate.

Dawn DeVries notes that preaching is about moving someone to have the experience of redemption.[51] This is possible because an experience that has been had can then be presented to others who are then moved to have the same experience. Of course, all of this presumes that the scriptural text is itself, in some fashion, productive.[52] The text functions as the occasion for the primary way by which the Word is encountered in Christianity via preaching, which above all else exists as a succession of Christ's own ministry.[53] The text is especially important in allowing us insight into the life of Jesus. For this reason, Schleiermacher assumes that preachers should prefer the New Testament as the basis for their homiletical work.[54] Terrence Tice sets this in context when he writes: "Christ's existence, communication, and influence compromise a 'natural fact,' one that is drawn in part from Judaic

---

und Unbefangenheit dies eine historisch wahre Bild von Jesus als dem Bringer des Evangeliums mit den von uns errungenen neuen Mögichkeiten unbegangenen sachlichen Ausdrucks, frei von aller Bindung an die Überlieferung, aufs neue zu zeichnen.")

51. DeVries, *Jesus Christ in the Preaching*, 59.

52. See Schleiermacher, *Hermeneutics and Criticism*, 3–8, where Schleiermacher notes that the task of hermeneutics, more generally understood, attends to textual construction and use, at both the universal and particular levels.

53. Tice, *Schleiermacher* (Abingdon), 68, 40.

54. DeVries, *Jesus Christ in the Preaching*, 55.

religion contained in the Hebrew Bible and in subsequent expressions, and yet Christianity is not to be explained by that prior religion as if Christianity could have developed naturally out of it, that is, without the distinctively new natural process that has taken place in Christ."[55] This attention to the new is important for many reasons. It demonstrates Schleiermacher's continuity with the historic church in the understanding Christianity as superlative in relation to Judaism. And so we note in the fourth sermon his disparaging comments regarding Judaism as a retrograde, if not dead, religion.[56]

For this reason, the translators have chosen to keep the term "Old Testament" throughout the texts that follow, in part out of accuracy in translation as well as an *aide de memoire* of the long-standing and dangerous Christian practice of understanding Judaism as superseded. To be sure, it needs to be affirmed that Schleiermacher did not understand Christianity alone as the sole participant in the *missio Dei*.[57] And yet, as per his *confrères* in theology and philosophy, Christianity remained a kind of consummate religion, even while Schleiermacher's vision was one in which redemption was to be inclusive of all humanity and all creation. More work, of course, needs to be done on Schleiermacher's relationship to Judaism, but in the interim an ethical imperative remains for readers of Schleiermacher to be mindful of the dangers of a Christianity that fails to keep its own biases and prejudices in check.[58] His theology has, however, self-correcting possibilities in his attention to the need of the exegete to read both Scripture and experience: "Schleiermacher openly speaks about the reciprocal interpenetration of the study of Scripture on the one hand, and on the other, of personal experience as the two decisive moments for the personal knowledge of Jesus Christ for every individual

---

55. Tice, *Schleiermacher* (Abingdon), 41.
56. See 78 below.
57. Tice, *Schleiermacher* (Fortress), 65.
58. A good beginning is found in Capetz, "Friedrich Schleiermacher on the Old Testament." Capetz notes the important contribution Schleiermacher makes in affirming the independence and integrity of Judaism, as opposed to viewing it as a *"preparation evangelii"* (303). He points out, however, that Schleiermacher's mistaken view of Judaism as nationalistic fails to consider its post-Christian development as well as Christianity as a Jewish sect in its nascent phase (304–6). A sort of essentialist perspective of religion is behind these assertions of Schleiermacher that Capetz rejects. He also calls us to take seriously the Jewishness of Jesus (314). This emphasis would enable Schleiermacher's historical affirmation of religious diversity to problematize his Christology and soteriology, as well as his vision of Christianity as an altogether new religion (317, 321).

Christian."⁵⁹ It is both ironic and telling that here we reference the work of Emmanuel Hirsch, a student of Schleiermacher whose anti-Semitism has tarnished his very own career and reputation. But still, it remains true that a corrective to our prejudices is found in a principle dearly held by Schleiermacher: our reading of Scripture is to be tempered by our attention to our experience, while the obverse obtains as well. Readers of these passion sermons will be challenged to discern how well Schleiermacher does precisely that as he attempts to make sense of the one of the greatest of enigmas of Christianity: the death of Jesus.

In what follows, a précis of each sermon is provided in preparation for the nine sermons proper.

The Nine Sermons

In the first sermon, preached on the first Sunday in Lent, March 11, 1832, on Luke 24:25, 26, Schleiermacher exegetes Luke's account of Jesus' upbraiding the disciples at the end of the walk to Emmaus.⁶⁰ He points out that "Oh, how foolish you are!" is followed by Jesus' "beginning with Moses . . . he interpreted to them the things about himself in all the scriptures." He begins by noting the unfathomable character of this event in which the Redeemer had to die at the hands of sinners. The text he treats resolves the seemingly intractable character of this theodicy by simply announcing it as necessary. This turns Schleiermacher to the question of the divine decree, which readers of his monograph on election know to be singular in nature and universal in sweep.⁶¹ In sum, all happens by a necessity that can finally be ordered to love.

The first section of this sermon is an exploration of the glory toward which Jesus' suffering drove him. Schleiermacher assumed that God's glory illumines suffering. He identified this glory with Jesus' God-consciousness

---

59. Hirsch, *Schleiermachers Christusglaube*, 104, 105. "Schleiermacher offen von dem gegenseitigen Sichdurchdringen einerseits des Studiums der Schrift und anderseits der persönlichen Erfahrung als den zwei Momenten spricht, die für die persönliche Erkenntnis Jesu Christi durch jeden einzelnen Christen bestimmend seien."

60. Although this sermon is not a passion sermon proper, it is included here insofar as it textually looks back at the cross even while it is preached in liturgical time anticipating the cross.

61. This latter resolves the tension between salvation and damnation by seeing the latter as a stage in the former, a point prominent in Schleiermacher's articulation of the suffering and glory serving as the backdrop to this.

so permeating his whole being that he never did anything other than seek and achieve the will of God. This glory was an existential fact of his life, ever present and always directive, not to be confused with a glory identified with postresurrection existence alone. It is revealed in his preaching in the Reign of God, which is now expanded to include the disciples in this activity in a new way. The same glory takes on a new modality and extension. This glory, conveyed in preaching, turns people from that which is slipping away and toward the eternal and divine. Christ's glory now becomes his presence in the spirit of all human beings. This glory, moreover, is ongoing as Christ continues to enter the hearts of the newly birthed faithful. All of this happens by means of proclamation, identified as the medium of redemption.

In the second half of the sermon, Schleiermacher discusses further this necessity, refusing to see it as necessary for faith, however, since the disciples believed in him before his crucifixion. Indeed, his scolding them in this narrative under review implies that Christ expected his disciples to have faith despite his death, not because of it. The resurrection appearance of Luke 24:25 is not identified as the reason for their *finally* coming to faith. Moreover, he does not announce, after the resurrection, his self-proclamation as having been made complete because of the resurrection. His insistence on the need to understand that the cross does not stand as a precondition for forgiveness is related to his insistence that God's love and justice cannot be understood as contradictory; rather, all of God's works are connected.

The second sermon in our collection is based on John 14:30–31 and was preached on the third Sunday in Lent, March 25, 1832. Jack C. Verheyden notes that it "would be difficult to exaggerate the confidence which Schleiermacher displays . . . in the reliability of the Johannine text."[62] He deemed it more historically accurate than the Synoptic Gospels in that it displays the greatest consistency—a precritical perspective on John that sits alongside some historical-critical judgements regarding John.[63] This passage directs the hearer to Jesus' resolve to continue towards his death, and yet not because of the power of evil, since it has no power over Jesus. The passage is ultimately leveraged to provide the hearer of the sermon with some sense of the contours of Jesus' obedience, which is deemed a reflection of his love for the Father.

---

62. Verheyden, "Introduction," xxxi.
63. Verheyden, "Introduction," xxxi.

Obedience presumes human agency, according to Schleiermacher, and agency presumes an accountability for sins of both commission and omission, an accountability shared by the Redeemer. Does this make Jesus' responsibility for sin universal in scope? This accountability is not deemed to be one that issues in a "messiah complex," (as the phrase is used today) since Jesus regularly skirts dangerous situations in his ministry. In the passion narrative, for instance, Jesus refuses to ignore charges from authorities since that refutation would make Jesus guilty of rebellion insofar as authorities were acting within their area of jurisdiction. Rather, he opts to face charges. Jesus here illustrates a life lived faithfully under the law, yet in a fashion whereby obedience to a higher law, that of faithfulness to his Father, now serves as a canon of love ordering all his actions.

Schleiermacher understood that obedience is how love takes shape, even while obedience might well exist where no love is present. And yet, he notes that the disciples do not follow in Jesus' way in every instance. Jesus seems to approve. How can this be? Following Paul and Luther, Schleiermacher notes that Jesus' dying to the law frees us from the law. But this relationship is not read as if it were a mere theory of atonement. The power of the law comes to its end—that is, its completion—by the believer's participation with and union in the life and death of the Redeemer. Faith is named as that which unites the believer to the Redeemer, and this faith initiates believers in a new covenant, hidden from time until the moment when this seed would finally bear fruit. And—to the dismay of those who see the perdurable character of the covenant with Israel—this bearing of fruit bespeaks the end of the old covenant.

It is important to note that in this sermon Schleiermacher underscores how Jesus' "Rise, let us be on our way!" leads to a discussion of the role of the Spirit and freedom. In considering this treatment, Schleiermacher points to the powerful metaphor of the vine and branches, using it to eradicate the identity of Israel as recipients of promise, a strategy at odds with Paul's own use of the vine metaphor in Romans. In this latter, Christians are reminded that they are guests on a host root, and that the health of the grafted branches depends utterly on a healthy olive tree rooted in the promises of God. Schleiermacher seems to indicate that Jesus replaces Israel to the end that Israel is no longer necessary.

The third sermon was preached on the fourth Sunday in Lent, April 1, 1832, and is based on John 16:32: "The hour is coming, indeed it has come, when you will be scattered, each one to his own home, and you will leave me alone. Yet I am not alone because the Father is with me."[64] This text gives Schleiermacher the occasion to reflect on the importance of community, which takes up the first half of this sermon.

The crisis of the cross seems to include the dissolution of the community around the Redeemer. For Schleiermacher's theology, with its accentuation upon the community as the locus for the communication of God-consciousness, this is an acute problem. He identifies this sense of alienation and its attendant confusion, which shatters community and increases a sense of isolation, with suffering. The phenomenon of being alone at the cross, then, becomes the occasion for discourse on the phenomenon of human suffering. Suffering is especially difficult as it comes with the sense that "no-one knows what I am going through." Being alone and isolated strikes us to our core.

Yet Schleiermacher seems to allow for the possibility of a kind of sympathy that answers this suffering, which is not only about being alone but, more importantly, about not being received—the very crux of Christ's experience on the cross. This was, of course, a *leitmotif* of the passion narrative. This was the darkness, but in this darkness shone light in that Christ's God-consciousness did not suffer extinction in this moment, and he was able to communicate this with those faithful few at his feet. Even at the cross, the community of the Redeemer persists.

The cross, then, becomes an instance—as explicated in the second half of the sermon—of the being-with of the Father with the Son, who is with those at the foot of the cross. A community radiates out from this moment of seeming alienation. God communicates community even at the cross, and here we have the passing over of the task of community formation from the Redeemer to the redeemed, through whom Christ now works. Schleiermacher, profoundly, has the whole human race in view as the members of this community of the redeemed. Schleiermacher is able to derive pastoral benefit from this incident as he notes: "However much our lives grow dark, we should have this from him, namely, that the Father is also always with us, and that we should accept everything that happens to us as in keeping with his decree with regard to the salvation of the world."[65] Schleiermacher is able to take this insight that the Father is with us and write it large, comforting his congregation with the certainty that those

---

64. All references to Scripture in the Introduction and in the translations of the nine sermons make use of the New Revised Standard Version, unless otherwise noted.

65. See 60 below.

darkest moments of being alone are a transient husk around a persistent kernel of the redemption of the elect: we are never truly alone, and all that happens will find its completion in God's Reign.

The fourth sermon in this collection was preached on the fourth Sunday in Lent, April 1, 1821, and is a meditation on Matthew 27:46, which quotes Psalm 22:1: "My God, my God why have you forsaken me?" This is a highly troubling passage for Schleiermacher, since the notion of God's forsaking the faithful is not deemed a possibility, and since Schleiermacher also confesses that Christ's God-consciousness is uninterrupted. His solution for the problem is that Christ had the whole context of the psalm in mind in quoting this one verse.[66] He seems to indicate that Jesus did not intend for others to hear this verse, which almost functioned as a kind of *aide de memoire* for Jesus of the psalm in its entirety. He is not at all content with an explanation that suggests that this passage is evidence that Christ had to suffer godforsakeness for us, since our faith itself comes from Christ's uninterrupted communion with God. Rather than seeing Jesus as the one who experiences hell in our stead, Schleiermacher views Jesus as the one in whom we experience what he experiences: that is, communion with God. This communion is variable for us on account of our brokenness, and yet Schleiermacher deems it a sign of sanctifying power that we become ever more at peace in our sense of communion with the divine.

In the second part of the sermon, Schleiermacher locates this utterance of Jesus more broadly as one pointing to his solidarity with human experience, in that it corresponds to Jesus' disappointment in his treatment by enemies and fickle friends. And yet, Schleiermacher iterates that Christ's constant God-consciousness illustrates another way of dealing with these experiences: in the mode of poise and certainty (as illustrated by the psalm in its entirety) rather than despondent lament. Above all, Jesus' illustrative hope in the face of despair has the collateral benefit of enabling us to express love for our neighbors in the midst of our suffering. Just as Jesus suffered for us, so our suffering is to foster sympathy for others among us. In short, we are invited to participate in the suffering of the Redeemer and in that suffering to speak not just the first verse of the psalm but the psalm in its entirety, given its firm confidence in God's provision for our every need.

---

66. Smith, *Matthew*, notes that "the early church saw in the sufferings of Jesus a perfect fulfillment not of the one line but of that entire psalm." See for instance Justin Martyr's "Dialogue with Trypho," chap. 99. See also Luz, *Studies in Matthew*, 345, "one can say that in the early church the words [from Matt 27:46] were read in a Johannine way, and in the Reformation in a Pauline way."

In the third section of this sermon Schleiermacher notes with precritical eyes how the psalms of old spoke so well to the experience of Christ. But he moves beyond the Christian appeal to Hebrew texts and notes that the ancient church authors also willingly drew upon expressions of wisdom found throughout their environs: "They were so permeated with the feeling that if an ancient saying still retained its positive power in very different times, in such a saying there certainly had to be something divine, and that even after centuries still had merit in guiding and supporting people's hearts and minds."[67] Noting with great joy that we are participants in the Spirit, who has been operative in the history of salvation, Schleiermacher also finds contentment in knowing that God has never forsaken humankind. There has ever and always been a witness to God's great love, known now to us in the Christ. Somewhat disturbing, however, within what is otherwise an encomium of Scripture is his assertion that "our Redeemer had before him only the writings of the Old Testament which of course belong to an imperfect time in which the Spirit of God, speaking to less receptive persons through much less than perfect instruments, was able to disclose the divine mysteries and reveal the being of God to people only in a physical and pictorial way."[68] This sounds harsh to those with ears attentive to the Tanakh as God's gift to the Jewish people. Despite his status as the father of liberal Protestant theology, Schleiermacher demonstrates himself an heir of some of its deep-seated prejudices even while he urges his hearers to cast "a trustworthy anchor into the firm foundation of that Word."[69] One of the last gifts of the dying Redeemer to his followers was the example of having Scripture on the tip of the tongue, always at the ready in times of need. Still, that he deemed the Redeemer to have had a Scripture inferior to ours, is surely something to give us pause.

The fifth sermon in our series was also preached on the fifth Sunday in Lent, April 8, 1821, and works through John 19:28–29, where Schleiermacher pays attention to Jesus' utterance "I thirst," a phrase of some importance in light of Jesus' self-identification as the source of living water in John 4 and 7. And while he is aware of the latter instances as pointing to Jesus' spiritual resources and the former instance to his physical need, it is the physical need that especially arouses his attention and so becomes the focus of the first part of the sermon.

67. See 77 below.
68. See 78 below.
69. See 79 below.

Important to Schleiermacher's exegesis of this text is his querying the notion that Jesus' physical suffering was the means by which redemption was achieved. If this were the case, then alleviation of this suffering would have been curious, and possibly problematic. This is not Schleiermacher's concern, and so he is able to approach this little phrase with a different kind of curiosity. He notes that in his ministry, Jesus neither seeks hardship nor seeks to burden people with his own needs, and yet, as appropriate, he does sometimes ask for help. Herein Jesus' behavior on the cross is consistent with this ministry prior to the passion. In part, this request for aid reflects his deep-seated desire to demonstrate that pious acts of self-deprivation are not needed to commune with God.

He also compares this state of thirst with that noted in Ps 22:16 and the lack of evidence that the psalmist found relief even while Jesus did. Jesus does not look to Scriptures for prophetic intimations of how his life is to be lived but derives from them commandments of life that are exemplary for us as well. This latter is important as a corrective for Christians in search of hidden meaning in texts.

In the second part of the sermon, Schleiermacher draws heavily upon the fact that the recipients of this request would have been mercenaries or enemies of Jesus. And while we might imagine a resolute refusal to seek help from such people, he sees in this request a way of being congruous with his prayer for forgiveness for these who "do not know what they are doing" (Luke 23:43a). Moreover, he sees in this simple request an expression of God's ordering of the world in such a way that we live in communities of interdependence. Further, he makes much of the fact that refusal of help and refusal to help are two sides of the same coin, and so there is a certain divine imperative to draw upon this interdependence in love of neighbor.

In the third part of the sermon he further notes that Jesus' request for help was not made in the sure conviction that help would be offered. Just as towns and villages refused the help he offered, so the soldier could well refuse the help he requested. In both instances the phenomena of help proffered and help requested reveal the hearts of those with whom he interacts. That one mercenary offers him drink illustrates that the divine being united wholly with the human Jesus finds instantiations in even the most depraved. Hence, Schleiermacher invites us to ponder how people's supposed enmity toward us is always with mixed motives so that "carefully considered there is really no such thing as enmity to the good."[70] The good, although sometimes

---

70. See 94 below.

mistakenly understood, is finally the most powerful operation in the lives of collective humanity and will gain the upper hand.

In the sixth sermon, based on John 19:30a and preached on Palm Sunday, April 15, 1821, Schleiermacher's attention is drawn toward the small but potent utterance of Jesus: "It is finished." He sees a kind of parity between this and the "I thirst" sentence: both drawing together the manner in which God's will for humankind is being worked out. And so Schleiermacher notes the need to see "It is finished" as anticipatory since the work of redemption accomplished in Christ awaits justification, which will be worked out in the lives of persons of faith (Rom 4:25):

> Hence, if in the moment of his death he could in this sense say "it is finished," he must be reflecting on his death in the context of this limitless interconnection which begins with the first promise that was given to fallen human beings about the seed of the woman and that extends forward to that endlessness when he will also bring to the Father all those whom the Father had given him so that they will share in the praise and in the glory with which he had been crowned. Now certainly this is also completely true.[71]

He first unpacks this understanding in the first part of the sermon by underscoring that "it is finished" is manifestly nonsense for any who anticipated a triumphant instantiation of glory on earth. The "It is finished" is finally a reference to scriptural promises having been fulfilled in Jesus. Yet, since this fulfillment included his flesh and blood being nailed to the cross, it was not manifestly the case that Christ's work was only to be understood spiritually.

Further to the above, a key insight gained from this language of completion is the recognition that insofar as the work of Christ is first spiritual, it is dependent on the Father for completion. The same is true for us. The divine decree is at work throughout our activity, and it "is fulfilled by means of the deeply hidden interlocking of all times and all space, and one day must tell it to another, the earth tell it to heaven and again heaven to earth."[72] Just as John once said "He must increase, but I must decrease,"[73] so Schleiermacher sees this "It is finished" as a deferral of the Son to the

---

71. See 96, 97 below.
72. See 101 below.
73. John 3:30.

Father, in concourse with Paul's own vision of the subjection of the Son to the Father to the end that "God may be all in all."[74]

In the second half of the sermon Schleiermacher correlates this "It is finished" to the high priestly prayer of John 17, which illustrates the Redeemer handing to the Father his handful of followers, kept in faith yet battered by the evil one and the trials of the world. "Finished" here does not mean that there is not yet more to be done. And just as this was true for the Redeemer, so it is true for us as well. Just as the work of Jesus is grounded in the work of the Father, so too we are God's "handiwork."[75] Just as the death of Christ was a turning point from a fulfillment of his own work that issued into a community of love that continues his work, so too our dying to what we collectively long for is taken up in the community that follows ours. The drama of redemption, it seems, is written into the ongoing history of the church as God works the divine will in accordance with the decree of salvation for all. And while the work being completed is God's, God's use of our particular characteristics in fulfilling this means that our mark is left on the resulting work. And although Christ alone perfectly bore the image of God, our own journey from cradle to grave is modulating in piety such that comfort at the end of our days will only be had by seeing God's constant hand at work in this. Moreover, these words "It is finished" are whispered by us as individuals, and by us as a community, both being expressions of the way that God is at work in the world for good.[76]

The basis for the seventh sermon, which was preached in the afternoon of Good Friday, April 20, 1821, is Luke 23:46. This passage recites Jesus' commendation of his spirit into the hands of the Father. In a precritical mode, Schleiermacher sees this passage as the last words of the Savior, which John failed to record. He considers it a word from the mouth of the Redeemer that is fully human in nature, and, in fact, one we can appropriate for ourselves. The first of half of the first part of the sermon is given over to considering this matter.

At death, Jesus in human authenticity, trustingly surrenders himself to the Father. Schleiermacher uses the term "omnipotence" to name that to which this life is surrendered, an omnipotence deemed operative in the lifelong journey of the faithful. In a fashion, death is the moment in which this power is acutely revealed in that at death a kind of opening to us of

---

74. 1 Cor 15:28.
75. Eph 2:10.
76. Rom 8:28.

reality occurs. In an intriguing paragraph he writes of the body being the bond that unites our soul to the rest of the world. As the body dissolves "the next eternal moment . . . holds the spirit fast and is at work in it."[77] This eternal moment allows a vision across the divide of death, yet it is a vision that allows the believer to discern the work of God on both sides of the divide of death. The hand of God remains a constant before and after the moment of death. Jesus' experience of death, then, differs from ours only in that he received it out of a God-consciousness wholly intact, while ours is fractured by sin. And yet, there is a fundamental concord between our experience and his in that both are ordered by God's eternal decree, which accords the Christian a distinct confidence. This confidence is mediated through Christ, who as the Way draws all to himself.

In the second half of this part of the sermon, Schleiermacher is attentive to the manner in which this rendering of the topic of death bespeaks the unity of all things as ordered by the decree of God. That Jesus was especially aware of this, and able to draw on this vision in his irenic dying awakens curiosity in the pious. Schleiermacher explores what it is that enables Jesus to leave this world with such serenity, and notes how Christ's pleading for the forgiveness of his executioners and his attention to the well-being of his mother are two words that settle his soul into the task of dying. He reminds us that being at one with God is of a piece with being at one with the world in which our living and our dying occur. He notes that death too affords us opportunity to be about the task of making peace, and bettering the world. Therefore it is an act in continuity with the acts that have made up our life. Dying, then, is a moment of living. This congruity means that living is a learning to die. Indeed, Schleiermacher speaks of the experiences of the pious of settling into its origin in eternity insofar as they take leave of the earthly things of life, which is, finally, what death is.

With the eighth sermon, preached on Good Friday, April 16, 1824, Schleiermacher turns to Hebrews 10:8–12, wherein the system of sacrifice et al. is replaced by the ministry of Jesus. The death of Jesus is deemed to be the turning point in this move from sacrifice to ministry. Further, "the end of all sacrifice" is also intended to exclude sacrifices integral to other religious systems.

In the first half of this sermon, Schleiermacher ponders how the death of Christ ends sacrifices that were viewed as memorials for sin. He points to the manner in which sacrifices were means whereby anxiety over sin

---

77. See 110 below.

was supposed to be overcome with the assurance of forgiveness. This was deemed to be a necessary on a recurring basis, and was usurped by the eternal or once-for-all character of the sacrifice of Christ. This shift from repetition to "once for all" bespeaks the superiority of Christ's sacrifice. But a larger problem with the former system looms: the system was deemed by Schleiermacher to address the sins of the individual.[78] By contrast his phenomenology of sin presumes that there is a deep interconnection between the actions of the person who sins and the person counted as one who seems not to sin. The sacrifice of Christ, then, exposes the systemic and interdependent character of sin in human community overall—that is sin in humankind. Further, the former view restricted sin to that which was external whereas Jesus' treatment of sinfulness turns to sin as a matter of the heart.[79] Taken together, these two views demonstrate that for Christians "genuine knowledge of sin is wholly derived from the perspective of the suffering and dying Redeemer."[80]

In the final part of this sermon, he turns his attention to how it is that Christ's death takes away sin. In sum, the answer to this age-old question turns on the theme of sharing in community with the Redeemer. Here, Schleiermacher envisions a participation in the human life of Christ. This participation is receptive to that spiritual power moving from the Redeemer to the person of faith, now through the kerygma in the context of Christian community. Schleiermacher nicely articulates the shape of this kerygma:

> Was it indeed not altogether natural that this striving had to develop and be guided into the right way when the Father revealed himself in the Son, when the divine Word became flesh, and when the teacher who shows the Father appeared in human form, when the divine love became visible in the glory of the only-begotten Son who is its image? And is it not indeed the case that the Son knew nothing else and lived in nothing other than this striving to share all that he had received with his brothers and sisters, and to draw everyone to himself and into his life as being fully one with the Father?[81]

---

78. This view is considered by many to be an unfair reading of the sacrificial system, which also addressed particular sins of a communal nature. See Lev 16:15–19.

79. Here again Schleiermacher will be interpreted as engaging in a rather superficial reading of Judaism. See Isa. 58:6–11.

80. See 122 below.

81. See 126 below.

Schleiermacher notes how Christ continues still this quickening activity but now in community and via the ministry of the Word. The community is now the locus of "his singular life."[82] This life in community now becomes the life of the faithful, who lose consciousness of sin as they grow more deeply into the will of the Father. The faithful still battle sin, but sin is really rather seen as external even while present. For the person of faith, then, both consciousness of sin and fault (guilt for sin) are attenuated. The will of the person of faith is attuned to the Reign of God, and all that happens that is contrary to that will is not ascribed to the person of faith as such. This is not to gainsay the presence of sin within and external to such persons, but these are not accounted to them as they renounce participation in sin and embrace faith to the end of growing in Christ. Their fractured obedience is grounded in the obedience of Christ and so is satisfying.

The final sermon in this collection is based on Luke 23:44–49 and was preached in the morning on Good Friday, April 20, 1821. The text records the rending of the temple curtain. Of some consequence in this narrative of the crucifixion, for Schleiermacher, is the image that the darkness lasted until three in the afternoon, after which time it is anticipated that light would have returned. Two points are underscored in relationship to this phenomenon. First, he notes that the realms of nature and Spirit are intertwined, and "to discover this interconnection in the great course of the world's governance is the ultimate and highest goal of the most profound human knowledge and wisdom."[83]

This insight is informed by insistence on the theme of the singular decree, a decree that bridges both the spiritual and material and so locates Schleiermacher in that group of theologians who are able to affirm the value of the created order rather than to see it as a problem to be overcome. But secondly, his attention to this cosmic disturbance—followed by its reversal—is that he locates the "great turning point in history" precisely in this dying rather than simply in the incarnation or the resurrection. For Schleiermacher these latter two are really not alternate options but varied expressions of this singular instance that encompasses the whole of the ministry of the Redeemer. Something happens to humankind with the coming of Jesus, and in this sermon, he describes it as follows: "the heavenly light was

---

82. See 126 below.
83. See 134, 135 below.

now made innate in human nature."[84] This theme, too, has deep resonance with Schleiermacher's universalism.

Also important to Schleiermacher is the rending of the temple curtain, which marks the end of the Levitical priesthood, and what he understands to be a restricted access to the mysteries of God, which are now made available for all to see. Together, this ending of a special priesthood and the attendant opening of all to the will of God enable a confidence in the power of the gospel to reconcile.

In the second half of this final sermon, he pays attention both to those who mock and to those who stand at a distance from the cross. He notes that the former, as evidenced in the centurion, experience conversion at the sight of the equanimity of the Redeemer. Concerning those at a distance, he refrains from criticism, recognizing that these two groups will come to the cross in their own way at the right time. The cross, then, has become for Schleiermacher a powerful cipher, such that he can say, "'let us praise him anew for this faithfulness, and he will never cease to bless us from his cross on high."[85] This phrase may seem a bit odd to many readers of Schleiermacher, who might imagine his interest in the cross to be attenuated in light of his critique of traditional atonement theories, but readers are to be reminded that cross is an instantiation of the whole work of the Redeemer, and it cannot be thought in abstraction from his teaching, for instance; nor, indeed, is the opposite the case.

The present volume of sermons has been translated by Drs. Iain G. Nicol and Allen G. Jorgenson and dedicated to their students. The decision for this dedication was made at the bedside of Dr. Nicol in the ICU at the Peterborough Regional Health Centre. Shortly thereafter, on February 4, 2019, Iain died, and so ended a life of outstanding dedication to these same students (including Allen), their varying communities of faith, and the worlds in which Iain lived, on both sides of the Atlantic: in his native Scotland and his adopted Canada. His work continues, however, in his students variously shaped by his wit, wisdom, and love.

On January 10, 2020, Terrence N. Tice, who contributed the foreword to this volume, died as well. While we mourn their loss, we celebrate that the world is richer for their contributions to scholarship and beyond.

---

84. See 136 below.
85. See 142 below.

1

On the First Sunday of Lent

Invocavit, March 11, 1832

Hymns 187, 166[1]

Text: Luke: 24:25, 26

O, how foolish you are, and how slow of heart, to believe all that the prophets have declared! Was it not necessary that the Messiah should suffer these things and then enter into his glory?

My devout friends, every time we begin afresh this season of our Christian Year, which is devoted above all to the contemplation of the suffering Redeemer, we must ever again immerse ourselves in this depth of the divine wisdom, in this mystery of the divine guidance of our species that the Redeemer of the world had to endure the dissent of sinners and die at the hand of sinners, a decree that to the hearts and minds of Christians

---

1. Eds.—For this and the following sermons, the editors have made use of Schleiermacher, KGA and Tice, *Schleiermacher Sermons* in order to provide readers with a fuller background to the title, as ascribed in SW and shown above. This first sermon was preached at 9:00 a.m. on Invocavit Sunday (the Sunday after Ash Wednesday), March 11, 1832, in Holy Trinity Church, Berlin. It has been titled "The Divine Decree Regarding the Suffering and Death of the Redeemer in Connection with His Glory," The above noted hymns were located in *Berliner Gesangbuch*, ed. by F. D. E. Schleiermacher, 187, 166. The translated text is located in SW II.3 (1835), 216-28 and (1843), 216-28, this latter being the basis for the present translation. The sermon is also available in KGA III.13, 121-33.

seems unfathomable. Yet, with this in mind, what better kind of guidance can we have than such words as these, teaching us how on the first day of his resurrection the Redeemer himself after his suffering was behind him, looks back on it. Here, when he asks. "Was it not necessary that Christ should suffer all such things and enter into his glory?" there is expressed in these words the consciousness of a necessity. It was clear to him that it could not have been otherwise than it was. Yet neither for us nor for him is there any necessity other than the divine decree. Everything is as it is because the Eternal One has decreed that it be so. Nothing can be other than it is nor thought of as other than it is, because nothing can come to be other than only by his counsel and will. It is for this reason that in his words the Redeemer leads us back to this necessity that is grounded in the divine decree. This is the viewpoint from which we too should reflect on his suffering and his death, for this is the perspective that he himself specifies here for his disheartened disciples.

To be sure, the words of the Redeemer seem to contain something else. In that he says to his disciples: "How foolish you are, and how slow of heart to believe all that the prophets have declared"; and after he speaks these words of our text, the text adds further that he began to interpret the Scriptures to them "beginning with Moses and all the prophets." Of course, we can very easily arrive at the thought that the necessity of the Redeemer's suffering and death has its foundation in the foretelling of the prophets. However, my good friends, suppose that all prophecies having to do with the Redeemer of the world prove themselves to us to be of divine origin, and suppose for this reason we were to believe that no such prophecy has occurred in accordance with the will of human beings. Then, the surer we would be of this factor, the surer it would be precisely that the One from whom the prophecy comes is the same One from whom its fulfillment comes. Thus, suppose that we were to say that Christ therefore also had to suffer because this was what was foretold by the prophets of the Old Testament, and suppose that we also wanted to grant instantly that their words and portrayals were actually to have corresponded completely to what ensued, and suppose that in the suffering of the Redeemer we were to discover that everything was precisely as had been foretold. For all this, we would then be led no farther than to ask, "Why would they then have to prophesy regarding the Lord in this way?"

In this regard, the answer must be, first, that both prophecy and fulfillment have only one and the same foundation. Thus, because both prophecy's and fulfillment's one foundation was decided in the divine decree and because this was thus in accordance with eternal divine wisdom, this is the reason why it all had to happen in the way it did. That the prophecy preceded the event was simply a preliminary activity of divine love for the benefit of those who had to do with these prophecies, although the reason why it happened in this particular way and not otherwise cannot be contained in the prophecy itself.

This is why, my good friends, we must surely keep to the other words of the Lord. That is, when he says, "Was it not necessary that Christ should suffer such things and then enter into his glory?" he certainly did not wish that these two things should merely be set in juxtaposition, but rather he sought to establish an exact connection between suffering and glory in the same way as if he had said, "Was it not necessary that the Messiah should suffer these things in order to enter into his glory?" Could Christ in some other way have entered into his glory other than after he had suffered? This, then, is the way in which he reveals the divine decree to us concerning his suffering and his death in its interconnection with his glory.

Now, this is what we want to make the subject of our devout reflections. To this end, my devout friends, we shall surely have to answer the question as to what this glory of the Redeemer then actually consists in, and only then the second question, that is, as to how then his suffering has led to his glory.

I

Accordingly, we first ask, "What kind of glory, then, is this of which the Redeemer speaks saying that he has entered into it, and that in order to enter into this glory he has had to suffer and die?" To be sure, this question, my devout friends, seems to place us far removed from that to which we are closest, namely, above all from this arena of human affairs; because this is the usual way we portray to ourselves the existence of the Redeemer, his life here and his works, his suffering and death as a state of humiliation, his being taken up into heaven, and his departure from this earth and from this transitory world viewed as his exaltation and glory. Still, my good friends, when we consider the matter more closely and simply dismiss all those things that are derived from a completely different domain of our thinking and ask ourselves, "What sort of glory was this that the Lord had then gained and into which he first entered by again departing the arena of this earthly domain after his suffering and his death? How can this be? Is there some other and greater glory than that of an immediate union with God, the consciousness of which, to the extent that we are able to accompany him in his earthly life, he indeed never lost for one single moment?" Can anything greater be said of any human being than that one is at one with the Creator, with the eternal Father of all things and with all spirits as the Redeemer says of himself? Can there be a greater glory than the consciousness that so completely permeated him that he never did anything other nor sought to accomplish anything other than the will of his Father in heaven, but that he also truly and fully accomplished it and in this fulfillment of the divine will enjoyed an unclouded blessedness that nothing could disturb?

Surely, when we consider the matter in such a way we will then have to say that this glory of the Lord was everlasting, a glory that he did not lose throughout his life on earth; no human power could deprive him of it even for a single instant, nor did he experience its diminishment on account of either inward states or outward circumstances. His glory was always the same and remained the same so that he could not have entered into this glory for the first time after his suffering and death.

Even the disciples, to whom he spoke these words, may have been uncertain and doubtful like us, but they could not have remained so for more than a few hours until the later part of the evening of the same day. This is the case, for as they now returned to Jerusalem to tell his other disciples that the Lord had indeed risen and had just now even walked with them, the Lord then stood in the midst of them and then, when they saw him, spoke similar words to the disciples, who did not want to believe it but were still doubtful. Here he now says, "Was it not necessary that Christ should suffer and die and rise, and let repentance and forgiveness of sins be proclaimed in his name?"[2] Can we really say otherwise than what he says here, namely, "Was it not necessary that Christ should suffer and die and enter into his glory?" and place this alongside what he says there, namely, "Was it not necessary that Christ should suffer, die, and rise, and let repentance and forgiveness of sins be proclaimed in his name?"

However, my good friends, to which one of these two should we commit ourselves: to rising from the dead or to preaching about repentance and forgiveness of sin? Was the resurrection his glory? Was his glory this coming forth from the grave to assume human form again and to walk as a human being among human beings, to speak with them, and together

---

2. Eds.—See Luke 24:46, 47. Schleiermacher paraphrases these two verses here.

with them to accomplish everything that belongs to human life? In fact was this, in turn, nothing other than what had already been described to us, simply a service that he performed for his disciples, in that he let himself be seen among them again, and in that he spoke with them about the Reign of God, an addendum, a brief addendum to his previous life, a repeated departure from them? But his glory cannot have consisted in this! For this reason he leads us to the other option, namely, that in his name repentance and forgiveness of sins should be proclaimed to all nations beginning from Jerusalem.[3] This is the glory into which he entered, and into which he could enter only through suffering and death.

Now, my dear friends, in that repentance and forgiveness of sins was proclaimed in his name to all nations this was brought to fulfillment in his being given a name that is above every name,[4] for in whose name has such a thing ever happened? Moreover, what is greater than that which could happen in a name? What is greater than when in this same name repentance and forgiveness of sins are proclaimed? Preaching repentance involves a complete reversal of the human race from what is nothingness, transitory, and corruptible, to what is eternal and divine. Preaching the forgiveness of sins involves removal of every alienation of human beings from their Creator and Father, their return to a childlike love toward God, and unconstrained access to God as their Father in their every need. His glory consists in the fact that proclamation is in his name, and that faith comes from the proclamation, for what was proclaimed also arose from faith. This indeed is his glory. This is the glory that had already been extended to him during the time that he lived and walked on earth and of which he likewise says that, nevertheless, he could not enter into it other than through suffering and death. This is his glory: that he also is no longer a solitary human being on earth but lives in the innermost spirit of all human beings. As the apostle says, "it is no longer I who live, but it is Christ who lives in me."[5] This broadening of his life among the entire human race for whom and for whose sake he was made manifest, this powerful presence which stretches over the entirety of spiritual life on earth—Oh! Why indeed should he not call this his glory, the only glory into which he could still enter, because an inner glory could not arise anew for

---

3. Eds.—Luke 24:47.

4. Eds.—See Phil 1:9, Eph 1:21 and Ps 148:13 on exaltation of the Lord God's name. Throughout the New Testament this older practice is also transferred to God in Christ the Redeemer (see Isa 63:16); see also Acts 4:12 in this context.

5. Gal 2:20. Eds.—The verse continues "and the life I now live in the flesh I live by faith in the Son of God, who loved me and gave himself for me."

him, and there could be no greater inner excellence than that glory he had borne from the beginning and never lost.

Now then! My dear friends, he is still entering into this glory, for it is not yet consummated. Repentance and forgiveness of sins still have to be proclaimed in his name. Where they have already been proclaimed the proclamation still has to be spread further from one generation to another so that never and in no place will the mouths of men and women fall silent in speaking of Jesus as the Redeemer of the world. In all events, this proclamation still has to penetrate to places where it has not yet rung out. Since he has come as the light of the world,[6] he must illumine all regions that are still in darkness. Moreover, to this end everyone who has walked in the footsteps of his first disciples and who in faith has become his follower is and will again and again be summoned. This is so, for there is no faith without proclamation, just as there is no proclamation without faith. Hence, on the one hand, all of us must live in accordance with this glory and enjoy it together, but on the other hand we must also assist in bringing about this his glory. This is why it has to be of the utmost importance to us truly to understand the connection which he indicates here. Accordingly, let us now inquire about this in this second part of our reflections.

II

Yes, my good friends, given all that we have considered, we would indeed want to inquire into how it is that such suffering and death of the Redeemer would have to be the condition for this glory into which he is entering more fully into. However, as I talk with you now, I will not say whether any generally agreed upon answer to this question will be given, one which could satisfy everyone in the same way and in which precisely this mystery of the hidden decree would be fully disclosed. For who would want to assert this! Instead let each person not cease to seek and inquire, for in that process one would find an answer for oneself, an answer that would satisfy oneself and in which one's faith can rest. This would indeed be the sole condition under which each person, in turn, could also participate in the glory of the Lord and work on behalf of the glory of the Lord. Yet, my good friends, suppose that we consider how over so many centuries questions have already constantly been raised concerning the interconnection being considered here. Faith has ever looked to the cross of Christ. The heart has

---

6. Eds.—John 9:5 and Acts 26:18; see Rom 2:19.

ever found satisfaction in him who died for our sins and was raised for our justification.⁷ Still, it is also the case that however deep the feeling persons of faith might have, and however deep their hearts' innermost sensation, and however firm and unshakable faith might also have been from the very beginning onward, yet in their multiplicity, the tongues we speak were so distinctly separated from each other, the words were so different, so beyond the understanding of each other's language, that the result might look as if Christ were not a banner of salvation raised for all people to rally around, but were only a new Tower of Babel, at which the language of human beings were to become entangled and their community broken to pieces.⁸ Then, my good friends, it would be impossible for us to believe otherwise than that, on the one hand, all along certain things that were false and questionable must have become intermixed with the answers to this question, but also, on the other hand, that the matter itself would be something inexhaustible. As a result, even if all of those considerations were to be happily settled, a considerable variety of different efforts could be thought of that might bring to light the inner nature of this interconnection. Hence, with regard to both aspects of this interconnection, only a little can be discussed in the meager space afforded here.

First, however, let us set aside one matter that has often variously misled Christians in their thinking about this interconnection and in ways that are different from how the Redeemer could have intended it to be understood. Indeed, suppose that we should want simply to set forth warning signs about the way we make our faith known. Then we must do this not from human arbitrariness, and in turn we must not have this way of thinking or the view of an individual provide the basis for this effort. Rather, with full surety, we would be able to warn ourselves against anything that could disturb the unity of our conviction regarding the Redeemer and our hope in him.

For this purpose, let us then together pay closer attention to the words of the Lord whereby he explains to us the glory into which he has entered, namely, that repentance and forgiveness of sins are to be proclaimed in his name. It would then become very easy for us to think that the connection of his death to his glory would consist in this: that his death would be an indispensable condition of the forgiveness of sins or even a condition of faith in him which is in any case the true nature of repentance and the real

7. Eds.—Rom 4:25.
8. Eds.—See Acts 2:3.

beginning of every turnabout to a godly life. Moreover, this assertion must indeed be true if there is to be any such connection, but only in such a way that, as stated above, the unity of life and work in the entire existence of the Redeemer would not be disturbed. Now, my devout friends, so often we do hear it said that the death of the Redeemer became the condition of faith in him; not infrequently this notion is presented in such a way that it is as if through his death he had for the first time genuinely confirmed his own conviction about his teaching, and it was for this that he died. Then it is primarily this strength of his own conviction that became the ground of our faith. But how can this be so? Did his disciples not already believe in him during the time that he walked among them? Had he not acknowledged their faith as genuine, true, and pleasing to God, just as one of them spoke to him and said: "But we," (namely, after they had discussed with him what the people were saying about him), "but we have recognized and believed that you are truly Christ, the Son of the living God."[9] Did the Redeemer not declare such faith to be the real, complete and sufficient faith when he addressed the leading spokesman and said: "Blessed are you, Simon son of Jonah! For flesh and blood has not revealed this to you, but my Father in heaven."[10] Jesus was thus stamping his seal of goodwill on this faith in him already at that time, when his disciples had no idea of his death. Indeed, he himself did not refer them to his impending death at first, rather he did this just as their faith was expressing itself as an experience of the communication of eternal life through him in his life and work. Hence the Redeemer then said, "Flesh and blood has not revealed it to you, but my Father in heaven."

Moreover, here too, as elsewhere, he would have had to scold his disciples if his death were thought to be the primary basis of their faith![11] He did reproach them at that later point because they then wanted to stop believing, because their faith would be at the point of wavering on account of his death. This was the case, for this was how they spoke after they had told him what had taken place in Jerusalem. As they said: "we had hoped that he was the one to redeem Israel"[12]—as though their hope was then in the process of being extinguished. This is why he scolded them for their foolishness and slowness of heart. However, if their faith were to have been based primarily on his death, he would have to have

9. Eds.—Based on Matt 16:16.
10. Matt 16:17.
11. Eds.—Luke 24:25–26.
12. Eds.—Luke 24:21a.

said instead that "what you have believed about me until now, what you have taught, what you have thought, all of this was an empty semblance of the nature of faith, only now apparent after my suffering death. Only now have I become the object of your faith."

However, he could not either at that time or at any time have said anything of this sort to his disciples. Rather, when he did say to them, "Unless you eat the flesh of the Son of man and drink his blood you have no life in you,"[13] then at the same time he said to them, "The flesh is useless. The words that I have spoken to you are spirit and life." With regard to his flesh and blood he is not thinking of his death but simply and precisely of this intimate community of life they had with him.

Moreover, this can be expressed in no more exact way than as follows: that his disciples are nourished by him, that they live from him, and that through faith they shall receive the force of a pure and higher life. However, in this relation he never thought of death as being the necessary first point of contact for forming this new bond of faith. If this had been the case, in this respect his own self-proclamation would have been incomplete. Also, after his death he made no use of the opportunity afforded him by the resurrection to complete his self-proclamation, because during the days of his resurrection he had nothing to say regarding this matter.

A second matter is also to be considered. When the Redeemer said: "It was necessary that I should suffer and die so that repentance and forgiveness of sins would be proclaimed in my name," we might then think that in this sense his death would be the condition of the forgiveness of sins, also that apart from it and without such a death of the Redeemer sin would not have been forgiven. How easily, my good friends, does this supposition introduce an insoluble confusion into our notions of the Supreme Being! How we must guard ourselves against viewing the love of our heavenly Father and the justice of the eternal God as two contradictory sides of his being such that the one draws to itself what the other thrusts away from itself, as if love were to open its arms to embrace the lost children and justice were to know when to open them only to let the sword crash upon the head of the sinner! There is indeed a connection between the death of the sinner and the forgiveness of sins because in an unfathomable manner everything in this great work of God is interconnected. However, we could all too easily seek to combine the two in such a way that we would sooner lose the firm basis of faith than establish it more securely by such means. "Jesus Christ is

---

13. Eds.—John 6:63.

the same, yesterday, today and forever."[14] We have to think of this and hold firmly to it; when Jesus Christ lived on earth he was already the source of the spiritual life for all human beings. In the same way that he was this source before he was yet to die for all human beings, he also directly apportioned this life, directly opening the eyes of the spirit for his disciples so that they could behold the restoration of the community between heaven and earth, as though with bodily eyes they could see God's good pleasure in his Son. And today, after he died and rose, was taken up into heaven and exalted above the arena of this world, this same Jesus Christ bequeathed to us the words of life, words that will not be made silent until the end of days. He is the One from whom alone we can still draw life just as directly as though he had not yet died, from him alone and entirely from him.

Now then, my dear friends, let us now inquire further. We might want to say, "Well and good, but how are we to explain this interconnection between the death of the Redeemer and his glory into which he was still to be entering?" At the outset, I would like to say that in this regard the death of the Redeemer is really not the issue. If he became a human being as we are, and if like children he took on flesh and blood, then on account of his earthly life he was also destined to die, for his life would otherwise not have been a human life, not like ours but an alien life. Thus, when the Redeemer said, "Was it not necessary that Christ should suffer such things and enter into his glory?" what he was referring to is the manner of his death. Now, in this regard two things above all tend to cause us astonishment. Concerning both of these things we would very much like to think differently had the situation been different: moreover, we would nevertheless always feel the necessity of its not having been different from what it was. The first cause for astonishment, my good friends, is this: that after his death the Redeemer again had to depart earth's arena so soon. The other cause of astonishment is that unlike the greater portion of human beings he did not have to die on account of the complexities of the bodily nature of our life, but rather that it would be necessary for him to die at the hand of sinners and be counted among offenders.[15]

The first cause of astonishment, my good friends, is indeed sometimes an object of our longing when in heartfelt satisfaction we sojourn and linger with him over the invaluable but all too few pages regarding the earthly life of the Redeemer. "Ah!" we think, "if only this life of the Redeemer had been

14. Eds.—Heb 13:8.
15. Eds.—Isa 53:12.

granted more time! If only still more words of heavenly wisdom had left his lips, some of them better to illuminate a certain matter that does not appear to us in its full light, others to answer yet a number of important questions that are always on the tip of our tongues and so as to retrieve in some a different context, ever anew, that same image of the Redeemer from whom we draw our lives." This, I say, is sometimes indeed the object of our longing, but when we properly consider this, we realize how little regarding this all too short life of the Lord was actually preserved for us in the few pages of the Gospel writings. Yet, even if it had been simply the will of the Highest that still more should have been put in writing regarding the life of the Redeemer, it would not have been necessary for him to live longer on that account. For he did actually say more, as his disciple states: he offered many more "signs, which are not written in this book,"[16] but what has been written is nevertheless sufficient to awaken and establish faith. Moreover, as to the Redeemer himself, how could it be that he—if I may express it in this way—was, as it were, impatient for his death! As he stated, "I came to bring fire to the earth, and how I wish it were already kindled!"[17] When, however, did it begin to burn? The answer is: not before that time when his disciples were going forth to proclaim repentance and forgiveness in his name, not before their words were penetrating the hearts of other human beings and arousing the need for a new life, with the result that the heavenly fire that he brought could now begin to ignite in the souls of those human beings.

This was the result, for what already began to move his disciples in their hearts and minds while he was still with them was indeed also the light and warmth of his life, but it was not yet the fire that could burn of itself. The Redeemer could have acquired more such disciples if he had lived longer, but, as he stated, "It is to your advantage that I go away, for if I do not go away, the Advocate will not come to you."[18] It was this Spirit that could make of the light a fire, and the Advocate could not come until Christ himself had departed the arena of this world. He would have won still more disciples had he lived longer, but the church, would have been born still later had he lived longer. As he said, "Unless a grain of wheat falls into the earth and dies, it remains just a single grain, but if it dies, it bears much fruit."[19]

---

16. Eds.—John 20:30.

17. Luke 12:49.

18. Eds.—Schleiermacher has: "the Comforter, the Holy Spirit" (*der Tröster der heilige Geist*) from John 16:7.

19. John 12:24.

This, my dear friends, is the reason why we have to view the earthly life of the Redeemer as such a matter of necessity, a life that was not to continue beyond the time when the goal had been reached. It is as if a sower would scatter seed on the ground and then depart.[20] Such was the heavenly sower, such was he who came and scattered the seed of the divine Word in human souls. He spread abroad much seed, yet only a few laid hold of his words, nevertheless with the result that then, in turn, he could and should depart the arena of this earth, and also on that account could remain no longer. Faith has been grounded within a few hearts and minds so that the fullness of the Spirit, the force from on high, could take possession of them, and so that the work of the Lord, his great historical process, could be further advanced without his being near them in person.

Now, my dear friends, let us consider the second cause of our astonishment. The Redeemer had to die at the hand of sinners. Enduring their opposition had to be the goal of his earthly life! Why would this be so? Why would someone holy be numbered among the evildoers? Why him, who had done nothing but good among human beings, and who was first betrayed by one of his own and then in the name of human justice put to death as an evildoer? At that scene, we would indeed want to cry out, "O the depth of the riches and wisdom and knowledge of God!"[21] Yet, if the Lord were to open our eyes, the same thing happens to us as happened to Elijah[22], concerning whom we are told that when God wanted to reveal Godself in an external manner, many other kinds of natural phenomena occurred in his presence. In contrast, he became aware that the Lord was not in these phenomena. It was only in "a gentle rustling" of the wind that he discerned the divine revelation.[23] In this kind of situation the same would happen to us, only in reverse. Just as there are many different forms of death, under different circumstances, at different stages in life—some sudden, some lingering—all of them gentle in comparison with this one. We will discern the Lord, however, in none of these otherwise than precisely in this violent death from which we would mostly shrink back in horror. We will discern the Lord only in this death from which there arises in us a deep inner feeling that tells us: yes, a time must come when no

---

20. Eds.—Schleiermacher paraphrases Mark 4:26 here.
21. Rom 11:33.
22. Eds.—For *jenem*.
23. Eds.—1 Kgs 19:9–14.

human being will any longer raise his or her hands against the life of one's brother or sister, even in the name of justice.

Yet, such a sacrificial death had to befall the Prince of Righteousness. How could this be? Can we think of him as dying in accordance with the process of nature, the clear eye of his spirit gradually being extinguished by aging or illness, and this occurring without an obscuring of his inspiring image? Indeed, for all that, how many forms of death, finer than this one, can there be! Suppose that someone, in full consciousness of his or her spiritual force, bids farewell to life. Who would not take this to be a good and great destiny of a person who knows how to elevate oneself so far above the usual frailty of human beings! What a rousing example this always is to us! How comforting it is when in the full consciousness of one's love one departs the arena of this world. When a pious heart and mind is touched by death we come to be aware of a childlike surrender to the will of God! Just so, moreover, even viewing such a natural death of the Redeemer could indeed still also sustain our enthusiasm, and in exactly the same way, in the final moments of the Redeemer's life, it could bring to mind the image of his divine life, if only the wicked hands of human beings had not taken his life away. Nevertheless, my good friends, we would have to admit that the full expression of his life occurred only in this death, and that only in this way are we able fully to recognize him. This is so, for he who was to bring forgiveness to all must have had so much to forgive, such love that even in the final moments of his life he had to have been able to bestow such a wealth of love, surrounded as he was by so much enmity and bitter hatred, and yet, the force of divine love in him must not have been the least bit disturbed.

Yes indeed, my good friends, this is the spell of the cross! If one may speak of a divine decree in the way we have here, it was on this account that it was worth all that trouble for Christ to die on the cross, which for the Jews was a scandal and for the Greeks foolishness.[24] Nevertheless, the scandal and the foolishness are both overcome when we begin to behold the glory of the only begotten Son. As a consequence, it is also precisely the cross of the Lord that becomes for all of us the real inspiration of life, the surest testimony of the fullness of blessedness that bursts forth and flows over us from him. This is so, precisely because the cross brings the fullest enjoyment and is the fullest revelation of the divine love working in and through him. This is why it is primarily in the event of the cross that for

---

24. Eds.—1 Cor 1:23.

us he becomes the full reflected splendor of the divine love. This is why he could not shine in his full light sooner, but only when in this way he was raised up as a sign. This is why he himself says, "And I, when I am lifted up from the earth will draw all people to myself."[25]

O, how blessed is the experience of all faithful souls who find their faith, ever anew, at the cross of the Redeemer—always there having the innermost feeling of the divine force that lived in him, always there having the fullest consciousness of the divine love that called sinners to himself, always there having the most mature faith such that no other can come who will excel this Redeemer in whose name and in no other salvation is granted to human beings.[26] There, in him, is the most immediate interconnection between his being raised up on the cross and his ascension into heaven. Indeed, my good friends, it was therefore fitting for the Father, who wanted to call many to blessedness, that he let the Duke of Blessedness[27] to be perfected by suffering death. Indeed, it was thus fitting for Jesus that "he was crowned with glory and honor because of the suffering of death."[28] Amen.

---

25. Eds.—John 12:32.
26. Eds.—Acts 4:12.
27. Eds.—". . . den Herzog der Seligkeit . . ."
28. Eds.—Heb 12:9–10.

2

The Disposition in Which Christ Faced His Suffering

A Passion Sermon, March 25, 1832[1]

Text. John 14:30–31

I will no longer talk much with you, for the ruler of this world is coming. He has no power over me; but I do as the Father has commanded me, so that the world may know that I love the Father. Rise, let us be on our way.

My devout friends, in our first reflection on the subject of Christ's suffering we chose the Lord's words from the days of his resurrection[2] when he had put his suffering behind him and as victor over death was now able to look back on it. We also considered how at that time he discussed with his disciples the interconnection and necessity of this divine decree. The words of the Redeemer in today's text are from the middle part of the context of his final discourse. He was about to go together with the disciples to the place where he knew that those who had been sent out to take him prisoner awaited him. He summoned them to rise from that place where they had held the last farewell meal with him. And here, my

---

1. This sermon was preached in Holy Trinity Church, Berlin on Oculi Sunday (the third Sunday in Lent), March 25, 1832, at 9:00 a.m. The hymn preceding the sermon was "An deine Leiden denken wir," which is found in *Berliner Gesangbuch* (#161). The sermon is found in SW II.2 (1843), 417–29, the textual basis for the present text. This sermon is also available in KGA III.13, 142–53.

2. Luke 24:25–26.

THE DISPOSITION IN WHICH CHRIST FACED HIS SUFFERING

good friends, in the words that we have just heard, he indicates to us the disposition in which he now went forth to face the suffering that was now imminent, in that he says, namely, "so that the world may know that I love the Father I do as the Father has commanded me." Now, therefore, in view of the fact that he went to face his suffering in the way he did, they needed first of all to recognize thereby his obedience to the Father, but also, secondly, something still more than this, namely, the utter extent and intensity of his love for the Father. Now, therefore, let us make these two matters the subject of our devout reflections.

I

First, my devout hearers, the Redeemer says that he does as the Father has commanded him, and for this reason he says, "Rise, let us be on our way."

The way in which these two matters are interrelated emerges clearly enough from all of the remaining details of this story as a whole. Certainly, obedience can be demonstrated above all and directly always only in that which a person is to do. It cannot be truly demonstrated in what simply befalls us. Hence, if somewhere, unexpectedly and unknowingly, the Redeemer were to be taken by surprise by his persecutors, as they indeed believed would be the case, this would be something that simply happened to him. He himself would have had no role in the matter and also could not have demonstrated his obedience thereby in any direct way. But now he says: "Rise, let us be on our way, for the ruler of this world is coming." Yet, as clear as this certainly is, on the one hand, if by his suffering the world is to recognize that the Redeemer does as his Father has commanded, then he really needs to accomplish something. On the other hand, precisely this is what is especially difficult. If this is not the case, we rightly ask ourselves, does not God entrust every person with one's own conscientiousness, understanding, and deliberations in relation to everything that belongs to the preservation of one's life and one's activity? Elsewhere, did the Redeemer not make it clear to people how much he would have liked to continue his activity further, however difficult it would be for him already at this point to part from his disciples? And, as soon as he thought of them, how he must have wished that at least this time this cup would indeed pass from him![3] Moreover, when he went to face those who came there to take him prisoner, even though he could have escaped from them unhindered, does

3. Eds.—Matt 26:39.

this not seem to give the impression that by his having ignored this universal obligation that we might uphold our calling? This is so, for this is an obligation that God has in fact imposed on all of us inasmuch as he will call us to account not only for that which we have actually done, but also for the way we have laid aside the precious but, nevertheless, so short a time of an earthly life, however long it may last, to contribute something towards the fulfillment of the divine will. Does it not give the impression that it is as if the Redeemer had ignored this command and therefore that he does not do what our Father had also commanded him to do?

Now, for this reason, in part mainly to avoid this difficulty, many Christians developed the illusion that it is as if the Redeemer were subject to a different law from that to which the rest of humanity is subject, as if a dark necessity prevailed, one to which not only he was subject but to a certain extent also his Father and ours in heaven, which would be in accordance with the great law of justice since God is surely the source of all justice. On account of this necessity Christ had to suffer in this way and not otherwise. However, as much as the opposite also seems to us to be the only proper option, this is the reason why Christ himself was no longer willing to maintain his true obedience to his Father.[4]

Nevertheless, my good friends, this also simply presents us with a new difficulty, for clearly enough it conflicts with the fact that in every respect Christ is the example[5] in whose footsteps we are to follow. But besides this, we also certainly know how at earlier stages he himself acted toward and in accordance with that great universal law and thereby took care of his life, and how more than once he avoided the wrath of his enemies, or is this not so? Do we not read how on different occasions the people became angry at his words and wanted to stone him,[6] and that he walked through the midst of them and withdrew when they sought to take his life?[7] How easily he also could have withdrawn from his enemies on this occasion and then thereafter also conduct himself in the same way as he had done before! Instead of going to the place where Judas and his band waited for him, every other way stood open to him. He had celebrated the Passover meal with his disciples—as the other gospels tell us although we find no account of this in ours. Hence,

---

4. Eds.—See Luke 22:42: "Father, if you are willing, remove this cup from me; yet not my will but yours be done."

5. Eds.—*Vorbild*.

6. Eds.—John 10:31.

7. Eds.—Luke 4:30.

the obligations that had summoned him to the holy city were fulfilled, and, resulting in a completely contrary outcome, he now could again leave them and thereby also escape his enemies. But, in this case, why did he act quite differently? Why did he go forth to meet them precisely in the place where they sought him, where he had to fall under their power and thereby himself play an active part in this decision of his earthly life?

Now, the key to this situation, my good friends, lies in the preceding words of the Redeemer, namely, "The ruler of this world is coming. He has no power over me,"[8] for until now he had not come in order to accuse him of anything. If it had been an unruly mob of people that provoked him, this would have been a lawless power. When confronted with that power he would not only have had the right to withdraw just as he also actually did, but rather it would also have been his duty to do so. When some of the high priests or members of the high council sent out their servants to seize him, he nevertheless withstood them and did not withdraw from them. But his hour had not yet come, and for this reason, grasped by the power of his words, they did not dare lay a hand on him.[9]

However, now it was in fact the ruler of this world that came. This was the existing ordained power over everything concerning the worship and service of God, the law, and the sacred teaching of divine revelation. This power was allowed to pursue him. The persons who represented this power had reached the conclusion that Jesus of Nazareth should be taken prisoner and arraigned before the court. This is exactly why he says: "The ruler of this world is coming" but "he has no power over me"—"He has no power over me," or "he has nothing of which to accuse me." That is to say, he does not possess the power with respect to having any just claim upon me; that is, he has no power over me to the extent that he seeks to act merely in accordance with this power which should protect the divine ordinances and the divine law. But if on this occasion Christ had acted as he did earlier under different circumstances, and if he had withdrawn from those who were sent out, then he indeed would have given the impression of a person who refused to come before the court when summoned to do so. Had he done this, he would have let his life be judged according to the law under which he actually stood, and, in this respect the ruler of this world certainly would have had something to bring against such a person. But since, according to his own testimony, he was sent only to the lost sheep of the house of

8. Eds.—John 14:30.
9. Eds.—John 7:30, 8:20.

Israel,[10] on account of the mission[11] which he had accepted, he was not authorized to cross the boundaries of the region in which that power was binding and held sway. Therefore, in this instance he certainly could have avoided crossing those boundaries, but even if he were to go to some place within the boundaries of the area in which his mission had placed him, a place in which he had also wished to remain, this power would always have found him. Besides this, his seeking to avoid their demands could always become a rebuke and a burden to him, and, at that point the ruler of this world would truly have had power over him.

Now, no one should cause these pillars of all human order and obedience towards those in authority to be shaken, since it is on these that all kinds of human well-being are based. Without the sacred authority of established powers, without the power of the law, without the overwhelming feeling of everything else to which all people have to accommodate themselves, in no respect can there be an ordered human life. But wherever such a power exists, no matter how innocent one may be, it has power over everyone who seeks to avoid the law. It has the power to assess one's conduct, to measure one's actions according to the standard of the law, and to make judgments with regard to one's actions. The Redeemer was fully aware of his innocence. He was also well aware of the fact that his scattered adversaries would misuse the power granted them by the law, for, as we can see from earlier passages of our Gospel, this misuse had already been settled in that decision they had passed on him and about which he was informed. The responsibility for this action, however, did not lie with him. His duty was to submit to this authority, to the sacred countenance of the law, and not to shun those who were to administer it. In this respect, my good friends, he was therefore "under the law," as the apostle Paul rightly states in his Letter to the Galatians: "when the fullness of time had come, God sent his Son born . . . under the law."[12] On this understanding he had conducted his entire public life, for this was the divine decree concerning him that was already made known in the fact that he was born among the people of God. As important as this fact was, however, it is certainly not necessary to discuss it in this context, and it will not be discussed here. On this understanding he had consistently obeyed the law, had let himself be instructed in it in the years of his childhood and youth just as were others

---

10. Eds.—Matt 15:24.
11. Eds.—*Bestimmung*.
12. Gal 4:4.

from among his people, and according to the extent that he was instructed in that land he followed it most faithfully. Indeed, also as a teacher he constantly stated that he had not come to abolish the law but to fulfill it since he was under this same law.[13] In keeping with this obedience he conducted and lived his life in such a way that in the full self-understanding and spirit of his people—that is to say, in relation to the divine law in accordance with which the life of the people was ordered—he also could say: "Who among you can accuse me of any sin?"[14] Yet, precisely in regard to this obedience he also had stood behind those human ordinances that were later added to this law. This was due to his faithfulness, which, as is stated in another part of Scripture, he demonstrated in his being "faithful over God's house as a son,"[15] thus upholding the commands of his Father and submitted himself to them as an example to everyone. But since he also could not allow any human authority to be compared with that due to his Father and to his commandments, precisely because of this, at all times he boldly made it clearly evident that he did not consider himself to be bound to those human regulations. Moreover, although it would have been easy for him to observe them as well, in spite of the fact that he knew that precisely on account of his low estimation of their value he would bring upon himself the hatred of the powerful. Nevertheless, he even held it to be his duty, and not only his right, not to let himself be hemmed in by the regulations of the fathers and submit to them so that the divine law alone would mark the boundaries and the shape of his life and not some human word. It was precisely in this sense that he was always critical of those in power who sought to place human regulations on the same level as the divine law. He had scolded them about the burden that they laid on the people towards the law of his Father. Indeed the law itself was burden enough since in fact a great many of the circumstances that were related to those older regulations no longer existed.

This was how he conducted himself, and this is why he could rightly say: "The prince of this world has nothing of which to accuse me."[16] However, for this to be entirely true he also could not let himself attempt to avoid the investigation of those who had to administer the law. Hence, after such a decision had once been made against him it would also have been of no advantage to

13. Eds.—Matt 5:17.
14. Eds.—John 8:6a.
15. Heb 3:6.
16. Eds.—See John 14:30.

him to postpone the proceedings inasmuch as he had no knowledge of what it was that they had decided against him. However, when they later came to lay hold of him he rather had to present himself before them and could ask them why they had summoned this power, for he had certainly always been present there to make himself available to them.

Therefore, it was nothing other than complete obedience to the divine decree that detained him within the domain of what had become this power hostile to him. Hence, it was by pure obedience to his Father that the Redeemer rose to confront those who had come to rob him of his freedom and that he did not evade what lay ahead of him. This is so, precisely because his conduct proceeded from the authority that also ruled over him and under which he was placed as a human being—as a member of his people. It would then have been entirely superfluous if on the basis of some source or another we were to believe that we have to search for still some other matter that will explain to us how the Redeemer regarded this going forth to face his suffering as an act of obedience that he demonstrated, and explain to us how he could say: "By this the world will know that I do this because the Father has so commanded."[17] It is the Father, he thought, who has placed me under the law. I have honored the law and kept it; in accordance with my powers I have defended its authority; and I now also freely surrender myself to any test it can apply to the ways in which I have acted in the conduct of my life.

II

Let us now turn to the second part of our reflections and inquire as to how, precisely in this way, the Redeemer also demonstrated that he loved his Father. Now, my dear friends, as the Redeemer here claims, by what means is love revealed in still some different and special way with regard to this relationship other than through obedience? What is the essence of childlike love other than obedience when its true, most intimate, and most direct expression is indeed in every respect obedience! Nevertheless, it is certainly something different. It is one thing to obey someone regarding the wholesomeness of that which is necessary simply on the basis of a lack of insight and on account of an indecisive heart and mind; it is another to obey, not exactly out of fear but on the basis of true and loyal obedience but, for all that, with a heart and mind that is still resistant because of the

---

17. Eds.—See John 14:31.

fact that one's understanding and desire are directed toward something other than what is commanded. Yet, if the latter still actually counts as obedience and belongs to obedience only no more than does the former, then good! This is so, because also in this relationship, as well as in obedience, love is demonstrated above all through the trust and confidence that the will of the one who commands is certainly good, and that the one who commands wills nothing other than wholeness and blessing. Therefore, the love of the Redeemer was also demonstrated through his glad consent to agree to this command of his Father and to embark on the way that led him to his death. It is in this way that the world is to know that he loves the Father. Moreover, we can best understand the whole purport of this consent when we recall first and foremost how the apostle Paul described the divine decree concerning the suffering and death of Christ in reference to the law itself and with to which these words of the Redeemer are certainly also related, and when we once again look back from this point over the whole context in which the words of our text were spoken.

What, then, according to the apostle Paul, was God's decree in relation to the law of the old covenant? According to it, must the Redeemer suffer and die through this law and in the name of this law? My dear friends, even if we remember well the words of the apostle regarding this matter—indeed on this account—this is not, perhaps, as immediately clear to us since that law is now so remote from our thoughts that it has become quite alien to us. Nevertheless, suppose that we situate ourselves in that period of time, and enter into the understanding of all those who, on the one hand, in heartfelt loyalty, love, and obedience attached themselves to the Redeemer, but on the other hand, remained subject to the law when they saw that he too presented himself as one who was placed under the law, and that he never transgressed its limits. Then the fact nevertheless remains that, as the Redeemer himself says, their calling was to go forth among all nations to make them disciples,[18] and in doing so they would find it impossible to be too particular with regard to the law. In view of this consideration we have to ask: "How then, could this transition have happened? How could the Lord's disciples, who were placed under the same law as he was, dissociate themselves from it, though certainly in a way different from him?" Of course, if the Redeemer himself had done it—when with his example he had preceded them, when he frequently declared and taught that the times of the law were past and its principles fulfilled, and that now we have

---

18. Eds.—Matt 28:19.

to do with a different life!—then they would readily have followed him to share his destiny! But as placed under the law he had to remain so. They, by contrast, and all those in whose hearts the will of God should and could be written had to free themselves from this constraint.

How could these two possibilities coexist? That they could coexist at that time comprises the very law of God of which in so many places the apostle Paul says it is "the mystery that was kept secret for long ages, but is now disclosed."[19] It is the divine decree which he describes for us out of the experience of his own heart, yet speaking also, at the same time, in the name of all disciples he writes about the matter in the following way: "For through the law I died to the law . . . I have been crucified with Christ, and it is no longer I who live, but it is Christ who lives in me."[20] This was the divine decree in relation to the same law of which and of its instruments the Redeemer says in our text: "The ruler of this world is coming. He has no power over me." Hence, precisely this divine decree, and the decree concerning his suffering and death, were one and the same. Only on account of the fact that he died through the law did it become possible for his disciples to be freed from the law. Only inasmuch as they, of course, viewed their lives as so completely one with his, as if they had been crucified with him, was it the case that exactly for this reason the power of the law over them had now come to an end. Thereby the promise that God had already given in earlier times now came not from the intervening law but through faith,[21] and through a living commitment to the One in whom they had recognized the glory and blessedness of the only-begotten Son of the Father. Accordingly, the Redeemer knew that through the law he had to die in order to break the power of the law and to demonstrate how little the true divine justice could be established by means of a decree in which such a contradiction between the spirit and the letter was possible.

Moreover, in this way he also demonstrated that the time of the old covenant had elapsed, and that that time had come when God wanted to make a new covenant, not with a single nation but by means of the one with the whole human race that had proceeded from the eternal Father. This was the divine decree from time immemorial which had, however, been hidden. Through this law the people of God had to be held together in obedience to and in the knowledge of the one God, a law that in all its literal exactitude was

19. Rom 16:25, Col 1:26, 27.
20. Gal 2:19, 20.
21. Gal 3:13, 14.

a truly heavy yoke, one that often enough they indeed sought to avoid and sought to revert to idolatry, but only by means of such a yoke could they thus stay protected, and as separated from other nations, remain pure.

Accordingly, now that the time was fulfilled, God could send his Son who was born precisely among this people and placed under precisely this law. When he had carried his work to the point that when the grain of wheat was then buried in the ground it could do nothing other than bring forth much fruit. Then the law withered and fell away and more and more lost its authority from one day to the next. Then those whose Lord and Master had died through its ordinances were able to be freed from it. Then they could embark on a new beginning in the lively freedom of God's children, until among the deluded people confusion increasingly grew. Finally the point was reached when the external location of that old covenant had decayed. The temple was destroyed, and it became impossible to observe the law any longer. Then the Redeemer not only obeyed this decree but gave it his full and honest approval. He rejoiced in the divine wisdom that for the sake of his own he should become a curse and bear the curse of the law so that they would be set free from its bonds, and to this, his final task, he consented most joyfully to this hidden decree of his heavenly Father.

How well we understand this, my good friends, when we attend to the whole context from which the words of our text are taken! In a firm and resolute way, the Redeemer had to stem the flow of his words. Suddenly, he now had to tear himself away from the great many expressions of friendly and comforting assurances of God's love and from the beautiful and moving descriptions of the future so that he could say to his disciples that it was time to depart: "I will no longer talk much with you, for the ruler of this world is coming. He has no power over me; but I do as the Father has commanded me, so that the world may know that I love the Father. Rise, let us be on our way."[22] And as he then rose and left his place among them, he also again immediately gave free rein to the flow of his words and continued to speak in the same way as before. In this final hour in their company what glorious words he spoke! How he encouraged them in the words of our text as well as in those before and after them to demonstrate to them the glories of the time that was now approaching when he would no longer be present, but when the decree of his Father would be fulfilled and his earthly activity would have come to an end! How he aroused their longing for the victorious power of the Spirit which

---

22. Eds.—John 14:30, 31.

was to be poured out upon them and of which, as he states, they could not come into possession until he had departed from among them. Before this would take place, they would be unable to rejoice in the Spirit's supportive power in which they were to work for his Reign. Therefore, apart from the reason that was established in the circumstances of the law it was good for them that he then departed. Now that his words had caught on with them, they were to express themselves freely, developing his teaching and going forth as his disciples and servants. Henceforth, they would no longer need his external presence. Instead they were to understand his Spirit that was poured out on them to be his spiritual presence and on this account rejoice therein in a far deeper sense. And although in these words he did nothing other than direct the disciples wholly and completely to himself, to the divine power of eternal life that came forth from him, it was precisely in this way that they were freed from any confidence in anything else, in every false hope in anything except him or in preference to him such as might perhaps still be retained in their hearts.

When he had risen at a later hour in the evening and had left the place where they had met together, it was probably the objects that surrounded them on this final walk that called forth that glorious parable in which he is the vine and the disciples the branches. They were entirely dependent on him in such a way that only in relationship with him could they receive their power. They recalled that he had said to them that apart from him, there was nothing they could do that was pleasing to God, nor could they bring forth any fruit other than through him. He thereby warned them in this way against false confidence, traces of which could still have been present within them, against any confidence precisely in the old law, which for him had now become the source of death! He had pointed them entirely to the spiritual life that was to form the world of human beings into a wholly new, richer, and more inclusive domain of the divine presence! Moreover, in this knowledge, which was alive in him, which he sought to communicate to them, and which in this hour that for all of them must certainly have remained unforgettable, in this knowledge he spoke so deeply to their hearts, and he was planted there; and here, I believe, there most certainly lay the complete and full outpouring to the Father. Therefore, it was as God's image, as the reflected splendor of God's being that he made himself known to them. Thus, that which his Father had shown to him, namely, that he was one with the Father and that the Father dwelt in him in such a way that the Father was to be seen in him, it was in fact to this that he directed their attention as to the source of their new life in the future. And, inasmuch as he now perceived what would result from this event, how easy it must have been for him to go to the hour of his death! Of what little concern it must have been for him that he was now to die, that the grain of wheat had to be placed in the earth, in that his whole heart and mind of love was then filled with expectations of the glorious fruits of his death!

Still, the world certainly did not recognize this result at that time! There can be no doubt that he also knew this. Nevertheless he did speak to the disciples saying "I do as the Father has commanded me, so that the world may know that I love the Father. Rise, let us be on our way."[23] And for the fact that we know this, my good friends, we must above all thank the disciple of the Lord who alone preserved these precious and fragrant discourses from the heavenly Redeemer. Moreover, it is to our benefit that, on this understanding, what the Redeemer said with regard to this disciple during the days of his resurrection was to become especially true of him, namely, "If it is my will that he remain until I come, what is that to you?"[24] Hence, these accounts by this disciple who reclined on the Lord's breast certainly remain with us, and from the beginning they have always provided, for all Christians, the most lively image of the fullness of divine power in words from his mouth, emerging from his immediate life with the Redeemer. And, on the other hand, we have the precious words of that other apostle, who during his earthly life had probably not seen Jesus, or at least at that time did not know him as the Lord. This was he who after the Spirit had taken complete possession of him and who from that experience provided Christians with the clearest explanation of interconnections of the divine decree such that together with him we are astonished at the riches of the wisdom and knowledge in this divine guidance.

So led, the world has certainly always come to know more and more how Christ loved the Father and did what God had commanded him to do. And such is the love with which he loved us even unto death on the cross, which love now has truly become the source of all genuine human love for the Father. Indeed, he has led the children again to the Father; he, the eldest, the firstborn of all creation[25]—he, who by suffering death had to be crowned in order to open the way to blessedness for the whole human race. This is why, now we too, as belonging to this world that has

---

23. Eds.—John 14:31.
24. John 21:22.
25. Eds.—Col. 1:15b.

been blessed by him, seek ever more to learn to know, in his action, in his love, and in his death, true love and obedience to his Father, and in such love and obedience, with the result that then through the power of the Spirit, we may ever more become his disciples—we ourselves and those who will come after us, until the end of days. Amen.

3

On the Fourth Sunday of Lent

On *Laetare* Sunday

April 1, 1832

Hymns 164, 202[1]

Text: John 16:32

The hour is coming, indeed it has come, when you will be scattered, each one to his own home, and you will leave me alone. Yet I am not alone because the Father is with me.

M y devout friends, quite frequently in the course of these readings, from the conclusion of which our text is taken, the Redeemer had said to his disciples that he would not speak with them for much longer. But exactly for this reason and immediately before this he told them with absolute clarity that just as he had been sent into the world by the Father, the time had come for him also again to depart the world and go to the Father.[2] To his joy, the disciples had expressed their gladness at the candor of his words, and in spite of the fact that he now wanted to leave them

---

1. Eds.—This sermon was preached in the Parochialkirche, Berlin on Laetare Sunday (the fourth Sunday in Lent), April 1, 1832, at 9:00 a.m. The hymns, "Der am Kreuze ist meine Liebe" (164) and "Voll Liebe war, o Herr, dein Leben" (202) are found in *Berliner Gesangbuch* ed. by F. D. E. Schleiermacher. The textual basis for the translation is SW II.3 (1835), 229–38. This sermon is also available in KGA III.13, 154–63.

2. Eds.—John 16:28.

and return to his Father, they affirmed with certainty their belief that he had come from God.³ But just as they spoke these words informing him of their firm commitment to him, he exclaimed: At present you believe, "but the hour is coming, indeed it has come, when you will be scattered, each one to his home, and I will be left alone. Yet I am not alone because the Father is with me."

Let us now make this the subject of our reflection, namely, how here, and in accordance with this statement, the Redeemer openly points to his suffering which is now so near at hand, and let us ponder what he especially has to say about his situation during this time. Together, then, let us consider the fact of the loneliness of the Redeemer during his suffering. He himself describes it to us as follows, namely, that in relation to human beings he will be lonely and alone; but then secondly, that he will not be alone because the Father will be with him. Hence, to both of these matters, and with God's blessing and help, let us now direct out prayerful attention.

I

My devout hearers, when the Redeemer says to his disciples: "the time is coming when you will be scattered, each one to his home, and you will leave me alone," we are not to think that he says this to them as though he were rebuking them. Rather, in no respect does he describe this as their own action, as if it were dependent on their own free will. After all, what he says is that they will be scattered, each one to his own home. And so little was it his intention to reproach them about this matter that immediately after the words of our text he adds the word "this,"—that is, with the words that we have just heard in parenthesis, namely, "*This* have I said to you, so that you have peace in me."⁴ Moreover, at the same time he presents them as participants in his suffering. "In the world," he says, "you face persecution. But take courage; I have conquered the world, and now you will have peace."⁵ Therefore, inasmuch as he expresses this not simply in a general way but expressly says that the intention of these words of his is to instill peace in them, these words therefore were indeed words of his love and

---

3. Eds.—John 16:30.

4. Eds.—John 16:33a is here rendered using the editors' translation of the German in order to underscore the prominence of "solches," which is not clear in the NRSV.

5. Eds.—Note that Schleiermacher here inverts the order of John 16:33 so that the commendation of peace ends the verse.

not words of his disapproval. Of course! As this same evangelist tells us, he had also even encouraged and defended the fact that the disciples would be scattered. This is so, for when they came to take him prisoner he said to them: "if you are looking for me, let these men go."[6] Thus, it was certainly also unsurprising that as a result of this situation immediately confronting him, that his relationship with the disciples had to be interrupted. We are told that one from among them and his mother as well stood under his cross. But they were also only in relative proximity to him such that they were in no position to give thought either to any mutual spiritual communication or to any exchange of thoughts and feelings, and still much less to any other kind of assistance that they might have given him. And just as he was barely capable of speaking the one important and meaningful word to them—but which has come down to us—they were hardly able to hear it as in this way. Moreover, we are not told that they were able even to give him a single response. And then wherever the others may have been, even if they were also together, each of them was nevertheless scattered to his own home. The bond of their former union was torn apart. Each was alone with his doubts, for they had thought that he was to redeem Israel. But now, it certainly appeared to them that he lacked confidence with regard to this. Each was alone with his anxieties, doubting whether in some way his work could advance. Each was alone with his pain in view of the sudden, and for the disciples, so unexpected separation from their Lord and Master in spite of all the warnings and intimations in this regard.

Moreover, my dear friends, when we consider the matter carefully we have to say that there is nothing unusual even in this case. Rather, it is a common characteristic of suffering inasmuch as it separates and scatters people, each to one's own home, just as it is a characteristic of being active that it brings people together and unites them. Certainly, all of us always hear on every particular occasion that arises in the circle of our activity, not only a word from without as one of warning, but also a word from within as a voice from our heart that "weeps with those who weep."[7] But this is only a "weeping with," a "feeling with" the same condition and not really a "being one." "Weep for yourselves."[8] Who among you could, or even would want to, transfer one's condition to another person? Moreover, no one wants to do this. In every moment of the deepest pain we say to ourselves: "No one can

---

6. John 18:8b.
7. Eds.—Rom 12:15b.
8. Eds.—Luke 23:28b.

experience this as I do! No one can know how my heart is rent apart! No one is able to grasp this moment in my life in his or her consciousness!" This is because pain is always a submersion of the human being in oneself, and this is also not all that much different from those who from time to time weep with those who weep. Each person also has one's own ways and means of sympathizing even with the suffering of others. Yet nevertheless, what such gentle anxiety also often does is to stifle the most friendly and trusted voice because we well know that the difference between that which expresses our participation and that which the person oneself experiences is too great. On the other hand, when we want to pour out our hearts, as the soul demands, to communicate with others in the midst of suffering, this is certainly a work of love and activity so that here the sun of life rends the veil of cloud and again breaks forth. If we want to understand a person's heart and mind in the midst of a consciousness of what we have lost, this is certainly a call to action that comes from suffering. If we desire to inquire about such a person, the bond of common activity begins once again.

But the disciples cannot yet accept what they see so clearly in front of them. The shepherd is struck, and the sheep are already dispersed on that account. Therefore something else needs to come to their aid. Now this is the case precisely because this is the way of suffering, namely, that it causes a person to withdraw into oneself, and because all suffering is a form of submersion into oneself. Only such a submersion into oneself is actual suffering. For this reason we must never freely remain in this condition for any length of time. It is our destiny, and it is of the essence of our nature to live with others, through others, and for others. And this is why as soon as possible we have to burst the bonds that confine us to ourselves and that powerfully seek to hold us back within ourselves. It is certainly also only then, in the call to sympathy, that this first expression of action, that the new life begins again.

Nevertheless, my dear friends, how, then, could the Redeemer express this matter in such a general way when actually it applied only to his disciples? Since they would be scattered, each to his own home, was he for this reason forsaken by other people? Let us summarize the different moments beginning from the point when he was taken captive at night and robbed of his freedom by the band sent out against him, up to the moment of his last breath on the cross. What a throng of people surrounded him! Indeed, he was not alone for a single moment! And certainly he states it clearly, that when they would be scattered, each to his own home, then he would be left alone by them. In the midst of this crowd? Alone? Among this throng of people? What are we to make of this, my good friends? It is certainly not because of the proximity of people, and not because of their bodily presence that we are not alone. This refers to our being perceived and understood by them in such a way that our activity, which we seek to share with them, has an effect on them. This is how life among us is mutually shared. And it was exactly this that the Redeemer did not have in the hours of his suffering. Those men were sent out to him in the stillness of the night as though they were going to a robber and a murderer. He first had to remind them of how daily he had openly taught in the temple. They could not understand him and wanted nothing to do with him. The high priest and his associates, who, when they asked him if he was the Messiah and he affirmed this, saw in this answer nothing but a blasphemy. They could understand nothing about him. The pagan judge, however well-disposed he showed himself to be by rejecting with stern words the demands of the high priest, was still in no position to understand him. This was evident when he stated: "Certainly he is a king, and he has come in order to establish the Reign of truth." Those who stood around his cross scoffed at the thwarted earthly reign for which the misled crowd had wanted him to exert pressure but from which his soul was always far distant. What did they understand about the king of truth with the crown of thorns upon his head? In this respect he certainly was alone, and the less he was understood and comprehended the more distant all those who surrounded him were also excluded from all effective activity of Christ upon them. Indeed, his destiny stood out clearly before him confronting his soul even in the hours of his suffering. At that time he also knew well that his exalted goal was to fulfil the divine decree, and as always this goal was also constantly active in his soul as it worked further toward the salvation of human beings. How gladly would he have brought this about by means of the few words he was allowed to speak in the midst of his suffering, how readily would he have set them on the right way and led them to a consciousness of whether or not they understood what they were doing!

However, my dear friends, there must not and cannot be such loneliness as this any more. At that time the statement in its most profound sense was true: "the light shines in the darkness, and the darkness did not overcome it."[9] Indeed, the light of the divine love shone forth from him, the light that constituted the essence of his life. But with the exception of the two trusting

9. John 1:5.

souls who stood beneath his cross, it shone in vain. Nowhere was there a point at which it could penetrate the darkness so that from there its gentle reflection would shine upon him. This situation must not and cannot exist any longer, for since that time when the struggle of light with darkness reached this decisive point, the victory of the light has become more and more widespread. Now, when we know that "where two or three are gathered in his name, he is there among them,"[10] we can no longer stand there isolated from one another—no matter how often the opinions of the individual deviate from those of the others. He is in our midst so that the extension of his Reign can be advanced, and our participation in his activity is the indivisible bond uniting all those who have found salvation beneath his cross, and who are bound together in the service of the light. And as the shadows of the darkness become more and more mellow, so the light must spread more and more. More and more must human beings be sanctified in genuine and true love, and more and more must they be inwardly united in their actions against that darkness that at that time had reached its highest point.

II

Nevertheless, alone in the world's darkness the Redeemer was also to find comfort in the fact that he was certainly not alone because the Father was with him. This is the second matter for us to consider.

"Yet I am not alone," he says, "because the Father is with me." This "with me," as we well know, was heard as his voice, my dear friends, and not as that of someone else. It was the expression of the innermost union in which he stood in relation to the Father and in accordance with the fact that he could also say: "I and the Father are one,"[11] and with what he also stated, namely, "Whoever has seen me has seen the Father."[12] In the same sense he said that when the hours of the suffering that confront him will come, the Father will be with him. He would be abandoned by human beings and left alone only with regard to them, but not entirely alone, for as he says, "the Father is with me." Moreover, the ways in which he otherwise expresses this relationship of his differently, all of these together can also be comprised in these sayings. Consider how he says, not so unequivocally, that he is not able to do anything by himself, but only looks to the

---

10. Eds.—Schleiermacher has here rendered Matt 18:20 in the third person.
11. Eds.—John 10:30.
12. Eds.—John 14:9.

works of the Father, and the works which the Father shows him, these he does.[13] This describes the entire course of his life since the point in time when he appeared in public in the world. And his suffering which he now faced at that time, lay not in that time alone but was simply the apex of this life journey. Consider how he went forth to meet his enemies, was robbed of his freedom, was put on trial, made confession of the truth, was condemned to death and raised up on a cross. As was always the case in his life, and also now, there stood radiant before his soul the eternal decree of the Father directed toward the salvation of the human race. He knew that he was going forward to face the goal of his earthly activity. He knew, not only that at his coming the ruler of this world could find nothing of which to accuse him, but he also knew that even if he were cast out of the world, precisely his suffering and death would be the turning point for the destiny of the whole human race. And certainly, even the great closing statement, "It is finished,"[14] was simply the echo of this inward consciousness of the divine decree of eternal love that was fulfilled through him.

However, not only this, but also the Father's "being with him" was also a loving disposition and hence a quickening orientation of his mind and heart toward the whole human race even though in this situation he was surrounded by it only in its hostility towards him. But if the Father was with him the eyes of the Father were also on him, the eyes which illumined the world. Moreover, there were also present with him the conditions and laws according to which under God's providence the spiritual world is governed. Hence, his soul was filled with feelings as those of a father for his children, just as indeed his Father gave up his Son for the salvation of his lost children. Therefore in this respect, at that time and as always he was the world's intercessor before the Father, and the prayer "Father forgive them, for they do not know what they are doing,"[15] was simply the summary of his most profound understanding of the divine ordinances relating to the human race inasmuch as now the times of ignorance were past—but for which allowance should also be made—and humankind was now held together not under sin but by faith toward the end of days.

Still, the Father could not also be with him in any way other than at the same time through Christ's consciousness as the Father's only Son,

---

13. John 5:19, 20.
14. Eds.—John 19:30.
15. Eds.—Luke 23:34a.

"full of grace and truth."[16] The voice that was made audible to others only on special occasions in his life: "You are my Son, the Beloved; with you I am well pleased"[17] always sounded in his heart and was his innermost consciousness of himself. Therefore, in this love to him as the only-begotten One, the Father was with him in the hours of his suffering. Moreover, in this consciousness of the Father's love, how then did he still have a need for human comfort? For what sort of quickening did he have to long for from any single human relationship while he was conscious of this his relationship to his Father in heaven? And, my dear friends, is this not the legacy that we have received from him, as he says in his final prayer: "Father, I desire that those also, whom you have given me, may be with me where I am."[18] Hence, just as he was with the Father and the Father with him, this is also his prayer to the Father and his petition to him. Just as we at times, too, may perhaps be alone—as we often are when darkness surrounds us—so it was at that time when the whole intensity of spiritual darkening descended on Jesus, and the darkness of the surrounding night was only its weak reflection. However much our lives grow dark, we should have this from him, namely, that the Father is also always with us, and that we should accept everything that happens to us as in keeping with his decree with regard to the salvation of the world. All those who believe in the Son and who have devoted themselves to him in service also know that however inconspicuous their lives always are, and however modest their activity is, this nevertheless remains firm in relation to the decrees of the Father for the world's salvation. Therefore, just as we should always live in this consciousness as well as in the other which is equally important, so that if, on the one hand, Christ lives in us and we in him, on this account we also participate in the divine good pleasure. Accordingly, on the other hand, we are such persons as who through faith in him have received with him, the holy Son of God, the power to become the children of God. Hence, in every circumstance the Father is with us as he was with him.

However, my dear friends, there is still indeed one further matter that we should not overlook. The Father was certainly with him in such a way that in this moment his close presence was a comforting one. Was it not also precisely a decree of the divine love that as an exception to this great loneliness, and even in his suffering it brought individuals to

16. Eds.—John 1:14b.
17. Eds.—Luke 3:22b.
18. Eds.—John 17:24a.

him to whom he could declare his God-given peace and his undiminished love? He who with his love so often turned to individual persons, and now even at the cross an individual turned to him and pled with him to let him share in his salvation, and whose request was not made in vain! Moreover, when he was alone in his suffering, he was nevertheless able to see the disciple whom he loved together with his mother, and was able to bid farewell to them. For both of them that action was an inward bond for the entire remainder of their lives. And there is still more, my good friends; for from whence, then, come all these individual accounts from which in these days devoted to the suffering of the Redeemer we so often draw strength and edification; from whence come all these specific accounts of the individual events of these last days? The disciple who stood beneath his cross had not seen or understood everything. Moreover, we do not know how much all the others who were scattered each to his own home had seen of what had happened to their Lord and Master. But many of those who at that time were still enemies of the Redeemer may later have learned and experienced what they had done; and many, their souls set free from their delusion in such a way that they even let themselves be baptized in the name of the Lord. Whatever it was that they did not understand at that time became clear to them afterwards. And from how many others such as these might indeed the individual accounts that we read in the books of the evangelists have been composed!

Even though the Redeemer was surely not alone at that time, not even in the midst of not being understood by the people and in the midst of this anger that was incited on account of him, sanctifying influences—if not quite visible—went forth from him. Afterwards, therefore, many people arrived at an insight into the divine decree and had to turn around from their former delusion in order to become his disciples after he had previously been the object of their mockery. Moreover, my dear friends, is this not the story of the Reign of God that is ever and again renewed? Where it seems to grow dark and the power of evil gains the upper hand, where error stands before our eyes like a veil so that the sun cannot shine through, there are always better things in store and into the midst of conflicting passions the truth breaks in to forge ahead on its victorious way. If we simply have the right conviction of God's wisdom and love, we then see how that which is always better and more glorious is further extended, and everything that has happened in this way in the Reign of truth becomes for us a new surety for a beautiful and more glorious victory. This, my good friends, this is the word of admonition of the suffering Redeemer to all of us. Following him, let us also look nowhere else, not to the right, not to the left, but always only to the works that the Father shows us to do and which we see in his Son, in the deeds which he actually acted through and upon human beings. Then he too will always be with us, and even the days of suffering and sorrow, even the inevitable struggles of life, will ever more strengthen us in the faith that the Reign of the Lord cannot be overcome by the power of darkness inasmuch as the faith that is also active in our weakness, so that for those who love him, all things must also work together for good.[19] Amen.

God and Father of infinite goodness! Let not the memory of this day of the suffering of your Son on earth be in vain for us. Let us be confirmed in faith in your eternal Reign, grounded by him through his victory. Let us ever more earnestly and ever more as one single-mindedly dedicate all our powers to your service so that we may always sense the consciousness of your presence and nearness. On this account we pray to you in the name of the One whom you have ordained for our redemption, righteousness, wisdom, and sanctification.[20] Amen.

---

19. Eds.—Rom 8:28a.
20. Eds.—See 1 Cor 1:30.

4

On the Disposition of the Redeemer in His Final Hours

Passion Sermon, April 1, 1821[1]

Text: Matthew 27:46

And about three o'clock Jesus cried with a loud voice, "Eli, Eli, lama sabachthani," that is, "My God, my God, why have you forsaken me?"

My devout friends, it has certainly always been difficult for many devoted Christians to think of these words as coming from the mouth of the Redeemer. It is difficult to ascribe this to him, who at this same time—for it is not easy to decide exactly which of these sayings is prior in the sequence—was so clearly conscious of his divine power that he had received from above, that with the firmest conviction he, as the One who determines the outcome of the lives of human beings, was able to call to the sinner at his side and say to him, "Truly, I tell you, today you will be with me in paradise."[2] Moreover, at the same time this was he in whose inner life was the divine being. For as John tells us, God indeed is love, which was so powerfully proved to be the case. He petitioned precisely the Father, whom he also now addresses for forgiveness for his enemies; he, who in his

---

1. Eds.—This sermon was preached in Holy Trinity Church, Berlin on Laetare Sunday (the fourth Sunday in Lent), April 1, 1821 at 9:00 a.m. The textual basis for the translation is SW II.2 (1843), 399–416. This sermon is also available in KGA III.6, 570–87.

2. Eds.—Luke 23:43b.

final address to his disciples, fully aware of what confronted him, himself comforted them with regard to the human weaknesses they would show and then said to them, "And you will leave me alone. Yet I am not alone because the Father is with me."[3] Did he now suddenly change to such an extent that he felt himself now forsaken by the Father over whose nearness and presence he had rejoiced at that time in his inner being, and with whom he had always presented himself as completely one? Can this be so? This, in the very moment when he was on the point of completing the great work of blessing human beings through his death, for which purpose the Father had sent him into the world, and in whose immediate help he had always rejoiced! And how can it be that shortly thereafter, this godforsakenness must again have disappeared in such a way that filled with the feeling that he had finished his work and looking back on his entire earthly life with the deepest joy, he could cry out, "It is finished"?[4] How can it be that having given up the earthly body, he commends his spirit into the hands of the Father by whom he must now have felt he had just then been forsaken?[5]

How can we explain this? How can this be the case in him who constantly remained himself, whose inward communion with his Father in heaven was never interrupted for even a single moment, whose life also never could be interrupted if in every moment of it he was to be our Redeemer and hence the Son in whom the Father was well pleased? How can we explain such a change? How was it that his heart and mind became so cast down, having changed from the firm trust in the Father to the feeling of the despair of being forsaken by God? Indeed, also apart from the particular circumstances that I have just mentioned, when we consider the matter in and for itself, is it then true, can it then be true that God would ever forsake a person who is made in God's image? Could this God—who gave the following promise to the leader of his sinful people, namely, "I will not fail you nor forsake you"[6]—have forsaken the one person without sin, who was just as good in the moment of his death as he was at any time the reflection of God's glory? And if this was really impossible, can a consciousness of God that corresponded with what was not true in the divine being have moved in the soul of the Redeemer, who so often said of himself that he speaks and does nothing other than what he has seen and heard from

---

3. Eds.—John 16:32b.
4. Eds.—John 19:30b.
5. Eds.—See Luke 23:46.
6. Josh 1:5.

the Father? Is such a consciousness possible, toward which he, with his whole heart and mind, was directed in this moment, as was his word in the same way? My dear friends, it is impossible that we could think so! Rather, this constant inward communion seems to me to be most essentially and most intimately connected with our faith in the divine Redeemer. And so, our faith holds that this communion was always constant and without interruption—if indeed in this matter we may in human terms distinguish between a greater and a lesser—and this was most certainly the case, and above all in this moment when the only begotten and beloved of his Father in heaven left his call to live as a human for the sake of the sinful human race. Moreover, the plain understanding of Christians certainly finds little satisfaction in the artificial explanation that this godforsakenness belonged to that which Christ had to suffer for us.

This is so, for if he also placed himself in the position of sharing in the condition of sinners such as the man at his side who hung on the cross as well as in that of the many people around him going hither and thither—and if in this moment too he is also our Redeemer, he should therefore be distinguished from sinners. Therefore, indeed, he had to distinguish his own consciousness of himself from this compassion for sinners and hence that consciousness of feeling as though God had forsaken him could not have been formed in him in this way. This is so, because God does not really forsake the sinner, and it cannot have been necessary for our redemption that Christ should take upon himself anything that is untrue.

It is rather the case, my good friends, that we find the true explanation for all of this solely in the fact that the words of our text are not those of the Redeemer and not directly and originally the expression of his own situation. Rather, they are words of external origin which he simply transfers and applies to himself. They are derived from Psalm 22, which is an expression of deep human suffering, and which begins with these words. Moreover, only in connection with the entire content of the Psalm from which the words are taken and inasmuch as we always have before our eyes the fact the Redeemer simply transfers them to himself can we properly understand his meaning. Therefore, we shall now return to this and now guided by the proper source of the words of our text, we shall reflect on them with each other about what they make known to us of the disposition of the Redeemer's heart and mind in these final moments.

I

Now, in this connection the first matter to which I want to draw your Christian attentiveness is this: that when we examine the Psalm before us more closely, already from the application that the Redeemer makes of it, it is easy to see how little the death that he was about to suffer really meant for him; how slight the influence of the consciousness that the final moment was drawing near had on his disposition; and how little the feeling of its approach dominated his frame of mind.

Now, as I have already stated, in this Psalm—however much it is also an expression of profound human suffering—there is certainly nothing to indicate that the godly poet who describes his situation had deemed death to be immediately imminent or overwhelmingly probable. Rather, he describes himself as threatened by many dangers, tightly surrounded by powerful enemies, in various ways made fearful and mocked, and from every human point of view about to fall into the hands of these enemies. Yet, in the course of his complaints he nevertheless expresses the living hope that the Lord will rescue him from the sword and that he will still be able to praise him in the congregation. So, my good friends, if on account of its nearness the Redeemer had possibly been seized by the human fear of death, and if in such a situation he had also recalled the Psalm, then certainly the particular circumstances of the Psalmist's account could most appropriately be applied to those others precisely among whom he now found himself. But for him, these would have completely receded into the background in view of the great difference evident here, namely, that for that psalmist there was still a hope for life, one that powerfully stirred his soul, whereas for the Redeemer himself the moment of departure from the earth was immediately certain, and its approach had come near. Therefore, he would not have referred the words of our text to himself at all, or at least he would not have done so without properly emphasizing this difference.

This is certainly how all of us know in ourselves that we are capable of having such impressions. The more deeply we feel our suffering, the more we triumph in comparison, as it were, with such persons who also complain but who nevertheless have to suffer less than we do. If we simply imagine ourselves to be close to death—by no means do I speak mournfully, like those who have no hope—but indeed as always wanting to be filled with the joyous hope that at some future time we shall be united with him who has gone to prepare a place for us,[7] and if we also think of ourselves as human beings who have a sense of what our departure from this earthly life—so richly blessed by God—means, this life in which all our thinking and writing have also been pressed together with that in our lives which is directed toward the eternal; and if in this process we feel seized by the natural horror of death that already comes over us as we live with our image of it, then certainly we have to concede that then we would not choose such words of another person to express our inner condition. Such words, however, certainly in and of themselves portray the sadness of a burdened heart and mind yet in such a way that the development of the entire account reveals that the sufferer was powerfully supported by the hope of being restored to life and to life's well-being.

Hence, my good friends, on the basis of the application of this sacred Psalm that the Redeemer made to himself, we can certainly conclude that the difference was in no respect as important for him as it is for us, and that in this moment it was the enmity of human beings that he felt most painfully. But of his death he thought and felt just as clearly and calmly as we find this to be the case in those final discourses by means of which he sought to prepare his disciples for his death. "I came from the Father and have come into the world; again, I am leaving the world and going to the Father."[8] "A little while and you will no longer see me, and again a little while and you will see me."[9] Shortly before this the Lord was so calm with regard to his departure from this earth that in the consciousness of the living communion in which he stood in relationship to his heavenly Father, a relationship that not even death could change, he considered death to be of no account whatever. Moreover, since this was his authentic life, in this moment he also had to be calm when he faced his death, as he had always been calm before. And of course, in this respect, as in every other, he cannot be other than always himself.

Now, when it is a matter of death and certain other experiences, when the human heart is caught in the familiar oscillation between defiance and despair, when at the thought of our departure we are sometimes unable to guard ourselves against a feeling of anxiety that comes close enough to bordering on despair, then again soon after we look toward death with a clear joyousness that thereupon again turns to despair just when we believe that

---

7. Eds.—See John 14:2.
8. John 16:28.
9. John 16:16.

the opposite mood cannot now recur! What is the cause of this variation in the condition of our hearts and minds other than the fact that precisely within us too the communion of the soul with God is not always stable and the same, and that in this respect we distinguish ourselves to such a great extent from the Redeemer that the heavenly light, which now shines more brightly into our spirit then again in turn is made more obscure by human weakness. But this variation itself again exists in an inner interconnection with the sin under which all of us are held captive, and it was for this reason that it could not affect the One who was without sin. On the contrary, inasmuch as he voiced complaint—as the suffering person tends to complain—it was therefore granted to him to avail himself of the complaint of such a person for whom death still seemed distant, and thereby to show that its distance and nearness alike could do little to affect his soul.

My good friends, for the mortal human being it is a great good when day by day one becomes calmer with respect to this universal human destiny and in proportion to how one's end comes closer, one also learns to look forward with increasing calm and serenity to the soul's departure from this world. We look ahead, not as thanklessly indifferent to its genuine benefits and joys in which of course the all-powerful love of God is everywhere made known to us. Indeed, it is always with gladness that we leave everything that is behind us and therefore also every pure and spiritual enjoyment of life, and with every thought of our soul and every writing and thought of our hearts we strain forward to what lies ahead,[10] for this is the well-pleasing will of God, namely, our sanctification.[11]

Hence, if we become ever more like our Redeemer in the faithfulness in which in every moment of his life he fulfilled the will of his divine Father, precisely in this way we will come into possession of the peaceful and undisturbed communion with him inasmuch as according to his sacred promise in our keeping his word he comes with his Father to make his dwelling in our hearts. Otherwise, just as all temporal things perish, so also our own temporal passing steadily loses its weighty significance, and in calm equanimity we become ever more like our divine Redeemer.

---

10. Eds.—Phil 3:13b.

11. Eds.—1 Thess 4:3. This is our translation of Schleiermacher, who is here recalling a biblical passage but not quoting it exactly.

II

Secondly, as we consider these words let us observe the way in which the Redeemer shared with us the feeling of human pain and suffering, and hence, how he wanted to have all things that belong to human frailty in common with us, yet always only with the exception of sin.

In view of the fact that the Redeemer uttered these opening words of the 22nd Psalm, it is certain that the entire sacred psalm was present to his soul even though on account of increasing physical weakness he was able to express out loud only its beginning. Now, for most people among us it is of course a very common practice to recall individual statements from Scripture without at the same time having the context in which they belong definitely in mind. But in this way too the divine word affords us various blessings. Nevertheless, this is indeed always a very imperfect use that we make of it, and it would therefore be a much more perfect understanding, and also one that brings even more blessing—since every statement brings blessing only according to the measure of its clarity—if we could also always understand every edifying and instructive passage of Scripture in its whole context. But we can ascribe to the Redeemer the most perfect understanding of Scripture and also the liveliest remembrance of it. And inasmuch as he uttered the words of our text in accordance with the entire context of that Psalm, he also knew that these words in that context were not those of a despairing unbeliever who inwardly also felt that God the Lord was distant from him. In and of itself such a statement of complaint would most certainly have had no place among the sacred books of the Old Testament in which are included only those teachings, admonitions, and psalms of people who lived their lives in God's presence—people who had endured in the adversities of human life affecting them alone as well as those adversities that happened to their own people—who knew how to comfort them with his help.

Hence, we also read—directly according to the words of our text and to certain other similar exclamations—that this godly cantor continues as follows: "Yet you are holy, enthroned on the praises of Israel."[12] Therefore, in the midst of his suffering the Redeemer was conscious of God as the Holy One and was able recall the songs of praise of all those who from the most distant times had extolled the name of the God who was their deliverer and helper. If, indeed, the audible words were solely meant to be heard by him

---

12. Eds.—Ps 22:3.

alone, he could not have been conscious of having been forsaken by God. Therefore, we can relate his words only to some particular kind of complexity in his life, namely, that in his human expectations about the course of some peculiar circumstance this man of God found himself disappointed inasmuch as he was hard pressed by his enemies. And not only in this moment was he in no position to carry out his customary activities to the glory of the Lord, but for the immediate future he had to expect yet worse things to come. It is about this that he complains, namely, that in this exigency God had not granted his repeated prayer for help, and he expresses this in such a way as to say that his God has forsaken him. If, according to the entire context of the psalm, this is then the true content of our words here in this text, namely, that of the dominant disposition of a heart and mind, and if the Redeemer adopted and applied them to himself simply in this sense, then the fact that he uttered them opens up for us a deep insight into the condition of his own frame of mind.

Most certainly, all of us have had the experience of being affected in quite different ways by the complaints of our suffering brothers and sisters. Unfortunately we often hear from our brothers and sisters such complaints that arouse in us a deep pity, although the reason for it is not so much the suffering itself but rather the undignified way in which it is borne. This is a form of sympathy that cannot become a genuine compassion, and when it moves us we really have to be careful that it does not turn to disdain. On the other hand, there are also other complaints that upon our hearing them, do not so much weigh us down but rather elevate us so that with regard to these we sympathize less with the suffering on this occasion and much more with the glorious triumph of the Spirit over all suffering. And when we ask ourselves on what this difference of suffering is based, let us set aside that which in the first case had produced such an unpleasant feeling, and do this simply in order to remain focused on the Redeemer, who presents the other way of bearing suffering to us—in its highest possible perfection. This way is more perfect by far than that of the Psalmist whose words he employs. Hence, that which unquestionably is foremost and most essential with regard to this dignified mode of suffering is that which is eternal in the soul. It holds the upper hand over that which is transitory. It does not abandon faith in despair, nor does it abandon faith in anyone who from an external point of view seems to have forsaken it. Nor does it, from defiance, struggle with suffering without overcoming it. Therefore physical pain or the pressure of external circumstances are incapable of expelling thoughts of the Most High, but even in the midst of suffering the soul is gladdened and strengthened on account of the consciousness of God's glory.

Hence, the psalmist, lamenting the absence of external support of God, on which he had counted, nevertheless does rejoice that the Holy One lives enthroned on the songs of praise of Israel. This is so, for it is certain that the one cry is not intended to follow the other as though the first is meant to be refuted by the second. Rather, just as the thought is always swifter than the hand, when the psalmist wrote the first he also had the second already in mind so that complaining and rejoicing are not to be separated from each other. Therefore, of this we can be far more certain, namely, that the Redeemer, in whom one thought could never refute the other nor improve on it—although he spoke only those first words—already had in mind the entire sequence of the psalmist's thought, how it was consistent in itself, and how he could appropriate it for himself.

Now, if the psalmist brings to mind the glory of God by means of the daily songs of the people to which he also belonged, a people which also had the advantage of knowing the one God, albeit with the veil of Moses before their face, Christ in himself was able to think of much more glorious things: first of all, that the Father reigns enthroned upon the glorification of the Son, for indeed shortly prior to this he had given testimony in the prayer to his Father that he had glorified him on earth and revealed his name to human beings.[13] But he also heard the songs of praise of Israel. He heard the thankful praises of God, which from time immemorial referred to what had to take place in accordance with God's eternal and wise decrees: that the time would be fulfilled in which the Word became flesh, and that this moment would also be fulfilled in which the Redeemer could take leave of his life for the sake of the salvation of the world. He heard all of this: the thanksgiving of Abraham, who rejoiced that he would see his day;[14] the sacred songs of the prophets, who bore witness to him and who praised God concerning him who was to come; the moving voice of Simeon, who said, "now you are dismissing your servant in peace, according to your word, for my eyes have seen your salvation";[15] and the exultation of John, who deeply rejoiced at the voice of the bridegroom as the friend

13. John 17:4, 6. Eds.—This is our translation of Schleiermacher, who is not directly quoting the biblical texts.

14. John 8:56. Eds.—This is our translation of Schleiermacher, who is not directly quoting the biblical texts.

15. Eds.—Luke 2:29–30. Schleiermacher references verses 29 through 32 while only quoting 29 and 30.

of the bridegroom, and who gladly wanted to decrease so that he could increase.[16] These were the songs of praise of the spiritual Israel in the midst of which the Redeemer thought of his Father as enthroned even in the moment of this lament. And when with a better feeling, the psalmist states that he is more a worm than a human being, and when he complains about the mockery that he had endured and about the dangers that surrounded him, he indeed readily thinks of God's past blessings in that he says, "In you our ancestors trusted; they trusted, and you delivered them. To you they cried and they were saved."[17] Hence, the psalmist therefore had sufficient calm to reflect on the history of times past. How much more would the Redeemer do so, even while lamenting in the presence of his adversaries that it was he who appeared as the one who was forsaken by God? Nevertheless in this moment in the course of human affairs, this suffering was not to disappear without a trace (like the suffering of the psalmist), but this suffering was rather, above all others in this moment in human history suffering that brought to an end one period of world history and opened a new one. The Redeemer undoubtedly thought that all the blessings that God had demonstrated to any part of the fallen human race at any time were indeed nothing other than at most preparations for this one blessing in relation to which he was soon to express the conclusive word,[18] namely, "It is finished."[19] And when precisely in his confidence in God's compassion as inexhaustible and trustworthy, and simultaneously moved by a comforting hope the psalmist cries out, "You I will praise in the great congregation,"[20] adding, "All the ends of the earth shall remember and turn to the Lord, and all the families of the nations shall worship before him."[21] and does so in the same spiritual understanding in this moment, how could the Redeemer not have thought all the more of this glorious future that was near at hand? That is to say, how could the Redeemer not have thought not only of his Father and ours, but after this, of dwelling among his own and being present among them as the inexhaustible fountainhead of all spiritual life and all glorification of God in the congregation of believers? Through these believers' service a countless

---

16. John 3:29–32. Eds.—This is our translation of Schleiermacher who is not directly quoting the biblical text.

17. Eds.—Ps 22:4-5a.

18. Eds.—*besiegelnde Wort.*

19. Eds.—John 19:30.

20. Eds.—Schleiermacher here abridges Ps 22:22.

21. Eds.—Ps 22:27.

multitude of children from all the unbelieving families would be brought to glory like the sand by the sea and the dew at sunrise.

So, in the midst of feelings of the most agonizing pain and of the most profound humiliation he is filled with God and with the glory of his heavenly Reign. This is the perfect purging of all suffering in that so strengthened even the smallest trace of sin disappears and every power of sensory function's holding sway is broken so that the eye of the spirit remains free and the heart open for the great consummation of all things, guided and blessed by God, in which one's own suffering disappears like a drop in the ocean. This was the disposition of the Redeemer's heart and mind when he made these words of the psalmist his own, and it is to a likeness with this condition that we should also raise ourselves up. This is what the apostle also requires of us in that he calls upon us to "rejoice in the Lord always!"[22] This is so, for Christians were never far removed from all kinds of suffering, just as the apostle himself suffered as a prisoner, so that inevitably, with this "always," he too must have thought of the time of affliction. But in suffering, how can we rejoice in the suffering Redeemer if we do not also seek to become like him in this mode of suffering!

But there is still something else that appertains to the complete purification of suffering of which the Redeemer gives the best example. That is to say, just as love of God has the effect that in suffering we are also filled with a blissful remembrance of him, so too must the love for our brothers and sisters have the effect that in the midst of our own suffering, our compassion for their condition, of whatever kind it may be, should not die away. This should be so, for when someone in one's own suffering completely loses the sense of what has gone on around and about one and still goes on, when the most lively remembrance of great events in the distant past to which in the most natural way one is led to recall, do not enable a person to tear oneself away from all-consuming brooding on one's own pain; when a person refuses to weep with those who weep since on account of his own suffering he has enough to bear, or to rejoice with those who rejoice because he cannot require of a person that the happiness of another should make any impression on one until the oppression of his own burden will be taken from him—of such a person we certainly rightly judge that his being is all too deeply submerged in earthly things. If he offers the assurance that in his suffering he is mindful of God and that he will turn to God, then not without reason do we

---

22. Phil 4:4.

fear that this too is no genuine prayer "in spirit and truth."[23] Hence, when in our suffering we have God in our hearts then in our hearts there must also be love for "God is love."[24] Therefore, our hearts must be open to the whole world because the entire world is nothing other than the sum of the revelations of divine love, and this is why we also have to be able to become deeply engaged in all the joys and sufferings of others.

Other statements also bear witness to how during the hours of his suffering, the Redeemer proved himself to be faring. This is made clear from the words of our text especially in this way, namely, that these are not his own words but the words of another. It would not readily occur to any person who in an egotistical way is lost in a feeling of physical suffering to apply to himself what another sufferer has said. This is because he believes that no other suffering of the same kind can be compared with his, and when any comparison is presented to him he always knows that he can detect alleviating circumstances in the case of the other person and worsening circumstances with regard to his own. But the Redeemer gladly appropriates to himself that about which the Psalmist had complained, otherwise he could not have applied these words to himself. And to the extent that it was known to him, he enters into the whole context of the complaint and the suffering in spite of the fact that he could certainly say that the suffering of the psalmist was not to be compared with his own so that indeed in this way his experience appears to be completely in contrast to that egotistical tendency. But we discern more about this on account of the fact that the sufferer himself, whose words the Redeemer applied to himself, was also of the same mind as he and sought to ease his own condition by calling to mind the stories of his people as well as comparing much more unfamiliar experiences with his own. Hence, the Redeemer pursued these thoughts, and inasmuch as he appeared to have been forsaken by God he also rejoiced above all that through him, God was merciful to humans. And he most assuredly rejoiced in that here and there, he had caught sight of some of his own disciples. He also rejoiced that he had succeeded in preserving their freedom whereas he himself had been seized by his enemies.

Still, in order properly to appreciate the loving compassion of the Redeemer's soul, let us by no means forget the nature of the suffering he had to bear. Indeed, when human suffering has its source in the imperfections of earthly life, we rejoice and are uplifted thereby when, on the one hand,

---

23. Eds.—John 4:24.
24. Eds.—1 John 4:8.

the sufferer still inquires after the more fortunate person and, sharing in his joy, temporarily relieves his pain with the help of a bright smile. But also, on the other hand, we rejoice and are uplifted when those who love the sufferer himself seek to ease the sorrow of his heart, or to relieve the pain of a ravaged body, by an aching participation in the same suffering which he ponders. Those who suffer with him, perhaps on account of the same suffering which sighs after all consolation—such people necessarily lose sight of human help and of all the strength which is granted by a tender love. But a yet finer and more genuine demonstration seems to us to be this undiminished sharing in suffering when such is brought about by the ill will of human beings. This certainly was the case with regard to the suffering of that godly psalmist. This is so, for only all too easily in such cases there arises an explanation for this and even indeed an embittering of the heart if not toward human beings in general, then certainly toward everyone who stands in a closer relationship with those who have caused our pain. In this respect we rejoice that the psalmist makes note of the fact that God dwells in the midst of the praises of Israel, and that the Lord also saved his ancestors and delivered them. Moreover, since the enemies who threatened him themselves belonged to his own people, how natural was the remark that descendants to come would not be worthy of the help that God had shown to the ancestors, and that the people had not earned the privilege of being consecrated by the true God. But his enemies were also strangers, that is to say, heathens; hence, it is simply all the more impressive that, far from heaping ill-willed curses on their posterity as was the custom of his people, he rather rejoiced in the more distant time to come when the heathen would also worship God. In fact, how natural in this case would it also have been to express indifference and harshness toward his people. For his heathen enemies could hardly have threatened him so severely if among his own he had found sufficient readiness and support.

But how much was all of this outshone when, in his suffering, the Redeemer demonstrated his friendship with human beings! This is so, for not only had the leaders of his people united with the heathens but also with the people who so often were full of astonishment at his glorious deeds and full of enthusiasm for his teaching and yet had shouted "Crucify him!" Nevertheless, in view of his sympathetic remembrance of this psalm, he rejoiced in God's all-embracing compassion for the whole human race, a compassion sealed by his godforsakenness of that time and with a heart full of love, voluntarily suffered precisely for those who had brought about his suffering.

Hence, my good friends, if we are to suffer, let us then in this matter strive to participate in the suffering of Christ. As dwellers in this imperfect world, the things that happen to us that are the sufferings of this present time are not worthy of that glory.[25] Yet that glory can only be ours already here and now as long as we do not content ourselves with a miserable, isolated existence but rather when, by our living in and for others, the being of God which is love truly makes us into his temple. As Christians, what we have to suffer undeservedly on account of the world can become our adornment and our crown when it is understood to be the continuation and the complement of the sufferings of Christ. That is to say, our suffering complements the suffering of Christ when we are like him: without losing God from our hearts, and not letting the malice and scorn of the world be in a position to exhaust the power of love that is within us.

III

Finally, let us now also consider how in these words of the Redeemer he makes known to us his intimate knowledge of the sacred Scriptures of his people. Now, as I have already stated, the essential circumstances with regard to the suffering of the Redeemer were in every respect very different from the suffering of David when he composed this psalm. This suffering described in the psalm may also have happened to him at certain points in his life. It was chiefly only the external, less important circumstances of that psalm from which he took the words of our text that he was able to bring to mind. The psalmist states that powerful enemies had surrounded him, and wagging their heads said: "He cries to the Lord that he should help him and save him—how well-pleased he is with him!" Like the psalmist, although in much closer physical proximity, the Redeemer saw his enemies, yet did so with a wholly calm heart and mind since he himself had even begged forgiveness for them from his Father, even while beneath the cross they walked about and mocked him. He also saw that all of his trust, which he had always demonstrated, and that his inner communion, which he had always celebrated, could not prevent the outcome of his undertaking.

The psalmist complains about how the pressure of earthly suffering exhausts his strength, and how at the same time his soul is dried up and

25. Eds.—Rom 8:18.

withered in his body. And similarly, though certainly much more truly and deeply, this was precisely how the Redeemer felt after the long time he had hung outstretched of the cross, feeling that his lifeblood, deprived of its normal movement in its courses, was dried up, and that his life-giving powers had gradually become exhausted. The psalmist graphically portrays the certainty to which his enemies had already given themselves over inasmuch as he says, "They divided my clothes among themselves, and for my clothing they cast lots."[26] Moreover, this is also exactly what the Redeemer saw literally fulfilled with regard to himself by the hand of those coarse mercenaries who stood guard beneath his cross, and who now, in accordance with established custom, divided the small amount of booty among themselves. All of this, with regard to the cause and the ways and means of Christ's suffering, was really of no significance and the agreement between these contingencies and the statements of that psalm would have been overlooked but for the fact that in the midst of the suffering and indeed in the soul of the Redeemer, the memory of all the glorious words in that sacred book of the Old Testament was so alive. Accordingly, these particular circumstances were sufficient to recall the psalm of lament of that godly psalmist in such a way that now he made its words entirely his own.

My good friends, never and in no place has the Spirit of God left itself without a witness. Among all peoples, however far removed they may be from the clarity of our knowledge and the soundness of our faith, there have always been particular expressions of the divine in human beings which have been preserved from one generation to another so that from these yet later descendants have acquired wisdom and drawn courage. Indeed, teachers of old in the ancient Christian church also did not hesitate to treat heathen expressions with respect as an albeit gentle breath of the Spirit from above and to cite them along with texts from Holy Scripture. They were so permeated with the feeling that if an ancient saying still retained its positive power in very different times, in such a saying there certainly had to be something divine, and that even after centuries still had merit in guiding and supporting people's hearts and minds.

However, we Christians, who according to the Lord's promise have become participants in the divine Spirit, indeed rejoice in the certainty that with inexpressible sighs (cf. Rom 8:26) intercessions will be made by this Spirit for every person among us whenever anything within us moves us in such a way that the power of the human word is found inadequate to express

---

26. Eds.—Ps 22:18.

it. Nevertheless, this is also of great value to us in that from time immemorial there have been not a few people who, at least with regard to the gentler and hence more communicable movements of the heart and mind, were able to describe these movements to the rest of us in properly measured and instructive terms. For from well disciplined hearts they also were able to sing and play to the Lord, and with spirit and cheerfulness to cultivate the beautiful field of the shared praises of the people. The Christian church possesses and preserves such a great and glorious treasure of excellent hymns and expressions of this kind—without the divine Spirit how could they have been composed and articulated!—and our Evangelical Church in particular augments this treasure for the purpose of mutual use from century to century. We have not all made rich use of this treasure, but each person, according to the many or fewer of them that one keeps well in mind, knows how to bring them to life in recalling them in the hour of need.

But there is surely one matter about which we can certainly be of one mind and that is that the Word of God collected in our sacred books and now for such a long time made available to all Evangelical Christians indeed has a yet much greater power and in its own very unique way surpasses everything similar. With regard to those fine creations of Christian piety opinions are divided. Some of them are enjoyed by some people and for them this is salutary, yet for others they are less pleasing. But as far as Scripture is concerned the witness of all Christian hearts and minds is unanimous, and they pride themselves in the experiences that they derive from its sanctifying power in the midst of different circumstances. This is a power that cannot be compared with that of any human word. Indeed, all of us confirm that witness through our actions and cherish Scripture in placing our trust in it. This is so, for when one person wants to support another with advice and comfort in the distressing moments of life, it is then that no one knows of anything better to do than to seek to place before the soul of our brother or sister one of the many glorious texts of Scripture.

However, our Redeemer had before him only the writings of the Old Testament which of course belong to an imperfect time in which the Spirit of God, speaking to less receptive persons through much less than perfect instruments, was able to disclose the divine mysteries and reveal the being of God to people only in a physical and pictorial way. On the other hand, we possess a far purer knowledge of the divine mysteries and a completely direct expression of the divine wisdom and love in that which Christ, the Word made flesh, has spoken, and in that which his faithful and true disciples passed on to their contemporaries in accordance with Christ's understanding and as directly from his mouth. Hence, in spite of the fact that he possessed the witness to his Father in itself, and was in need of no other, the Redeemer nevertheless often appealed to Holy Scripture. He appealed to Scripture not only in his discourses but also in the moments of his most severe suffering. Here, for instance, he comforted himself with a psalm of lament despite the fact that drawing directly from the fullness of the being of God in himself, he would be better able to comfort and support himself—and that in ways more pleasing to God and more worthy of God. In such a way he could better speak for himself and to himself than in any other way to be found. But at the same time this was also a psalm of praise and encouragement from the sacred books of the Old Testament. And so therein, in an almost miraculous and gracious way, he sought at the same time to show us that he also for his own sake placed such special value on those writings from the land of his forebears, which already for centuries had been a sacred common property of all those pious people who had revered his Father. In the face of death, he did not disdain to call upon his Father in words from these writings. In the light of this important example, how would we not have to be yet more firmly bound to our Holy Scriptures of the New Testament, which of course contain not merely the shadow of good things to come like those of the Old Testament but rather the substance itself, which already for so much longer has proved itself to be the most powerful support and purest means of the refining of souls longing for salvation. This is so, inasmuch as on every saying from this source close to which believers have sheltered again and again there rests a special blessing of thankful remembrance. Moreover, just as we as individuals and also as in community are much too distant from the Redeemer to be directly satisfied by him in person, we simply all too easily risk the danger of losing our balance and suffering shipwreck if at the right time we do not succeed in casting a trustworthy anchor into the firm foundation of that Word.

Accordingly, may the dying Redeemer's example indeed be an new incentive to all of us always to maintain a lively knowledge of Scripture and certainly to extend this knowledge more and more so that it will not be necessary for us, as is the way with many pious Christians, to leave it to chance regarding how we will be guided when we have a need of comfort from Scripture. And so it will always be easy for us, out of the treasure of our own memory, to bring to mind that which it can impart to us and provide us with the most comfort, satisfaction, instruction, and good counsel.

Behold! The blessed Word of the Lord now embarks on a new and joyous flight. Conveyed in strange and, to a large extent, still unrefined languages, it hastens to the people who although they indeed have heard the name of the Redeemer and have become aware of some of the words of the language of Christianity, still could never have become acquainted with the story of the Redeemer and of the divine comfort of his teaching in this original context. May this in no way give the impression that perhaps we merely wanted to communicate nothing other than that Holy Scripture was of greatest value only for the earliest periods of faith and so left entirely to others as though we were no longer in need of it on account of the fact that the inward nature of our Christianity was so firmly based and so perfectly developed that we could easily dispense with the outward Word! May the impression also not be given as though the divine Word itself longs for us in our not being diligent and earnest enough in our use of it, that it has turned to others who would preserve this treasure as more precious, and that it could again mean to them what it meant to our ancestors. No, my dear friends! May this matter not turn into an exchange in which we can only lose! If we contribute our mite for the purpose of spreading Holy Scripture to every nation and people on earth, then at the same time it also has to become ever more effective among ourselves so that those laudable endeavors will constantly arise from the right motive, namely, that of our own abundant experience. Hence, in this matter let us also follow Christ's example, yet holding above all to the Scriptures of the New Testament so that the individual features of the image of Christ as well as his instructions to his followers will always and ever revive us so that the written Word becomes alive in our souls and in accordance with his promise bears fruit a hundred- and a thousandfold. Amen.

5

Passion Sermon[1]

April 8, 1821

Text: John 19:28–29

After this, when Jesus knew that all was now finished, he said (in order to fulfill the scripture), "I thirst." A jar full of sour wine was standing there. So they put a sponge full of the wine on a branch of hyssop and held it to his mouth.

My good friends, there is also among our Lord's last words from the cross this briefest and seemingly most insignificant one which he spoke just shortly before his end, namely, "I thirst." Nevertheless, this statement is seen to be particularly worth noting when we give it close consideration and pay attention to all the circumstances surrounding it. Only a few months prior to this, in the same great capital of his nation and in front of the gates of which he now suffered, among the festive gathering of thousands of people he had made the following invitation saying, "If anyone is thirsty let him come to me and drink of the living water."[2] And now here, we can certainly rightly say that he was about to make this invitation eternally valid in view of the fact that through obedience to death

---

1. Eds.—This sermon was preached in Holy Trinity Church, Berlin on Judica Sunday (the fifth Sunday in Lent), April 8, 1821, at 7:00 a.m. The textual basis for the translation is SW II.4 (1835) 342–56. This sermon is also available in KGA III.6, 588–601. A footnote is found at this point in the SW, indicating that this sermon is "out of the same series, as the previous."

2. Eds.—Schleiermacher here paraphrases John 7:37.

he was given power for all time to come to quench all the spiritual thirst of every human being. But even as he was about to bless the temporal gift and to bid the Spirit of his heavenly Father to do so, from a physical point of view he himself still nevertheless had to call out, "I thirst." However, it is not simply a question of us stopping at this contrast between spiritual fullness and physical need. Rather, with respect to the comparison of these two moments, what makes the greater impression on me is how with regard to the spiritual it was with the greatest composure that he offered them his spiritual riches and the fullness of the divine life. The spiritual riches and the fullness of the divine life in him were in him precisely for him to offer them. Also impressive is how he, with equal composure, admits the physical need, which he shares with everyone and makes known his need to be relieved of his thirst.

In the light of the prevailing circumstance, this open admission of his need becomes so remarkable that we now especially want to make this the subject of our consideration.

I

My good friends, because this admission is closely related to an important part of our Christian wisdom as well as to our Christian faith, what rightly has to come to mind in this connection first of all is this, that from these words that seem to have little content we indeed also see that to the final moment of his life our Redeemer never sought to bring pain and suffering on himself or took it upon himself as something meritorious. Moreover, just as little did he place the meritorious element of his work of redemption on our behalf in what he suffered. As you well know, with regard to the observations that are appropriate to this annual remembrance of Christ's suffering, I do not readily tend to linger especially much over the physical suffering of our Redeemer precisely because like all things physical such sufferings are simply the husk of the great importance of the event of his death. This is so, hence anyone who engages himself too long and too assiduously solely with this aspect of the matter can certainly very easily waste the true benefit of the inner divine kernel. But given this opportunity I have no choice but to draw our attention to the way in which the thirst that tormented the Redeemer was related to his other physical sufferings. It is surely evident that this feeling of thirst was slight in comparison with the sufferings and agonies which his outstretched body on the cross had to endure—in addition to everything else that had already contributed to his sufferings—specifically because of his being stretched out in this way. The sufferings and agonies were inseparable from the penalty of death to which his judges had sentenced him. Certainly, the thirst that tormented him also arose from the same circumstances, and of all the agonies that he felt on the cross he would not be relieved or even merely eased without again canceling the sentence of death itself. But since in his case this was what was decided, he endured with patient greatness of soul everything related to it that could not be avoided. Only with the help of human beings could this thirst be assuaged, and it was precisely for this reason that the Redeemer cried out, "I thirst," so that still even in this final moment of his life he did so with a view to receiving at least some relief from this unfortunate necessity with the help of human beings.

Now, if he himself had proceeded on the assumption that suffering was also integral to the significance and substance of his reconciling death and that with regard to it such suffering had to be endured: and if he himself had held the opinion that we find among many Christians, namely, by means of what he suffered the Redeemer had to cancel the sins of human beings in this way: that he endured everything that they themselves should have endured as punishment for their sins, and that for this purpose suffering could not be sufficient, then how, indeed, as he bore his suffering with patience could he then have been able to think about unburdening himself of even the slightest weight of this suffering in order to reduce it even by a little? And he bore this suffering in such a way that it certainly did not seem to him to be greater than it was—as if it was pervaded by the excess of human sin, which he had to bear on account of his divine purity. Hence, abandoning these physical notions, we also now turn to spiritual considerations in regard to this matter inasmuch as this utterance of Christ most definitely convinces us that the cup he had to empty to the last drop for our salvation was not the physical realities associated with death but rather the spiritual victory that he won. It was on this account that he himself was crowned with praise and honor in that he seized power from the one that possessed the power of death, and that by this means we were reconciled to God while we were still enemies.[3]

As we now see very clearly, he viewed this suffering connected with his death very differently from any other. So here we can also learn from him the proper way to do so, which consists precisely in this, namely, to bear the

---

3. Eds.—Rom 5:10.

inevitable with dignity and patience without becoming a burden to ourselves or to others, and for the sake of everything that can be alleviated by means of human help also to call upon that human help. Just as in his life we nowhere find that he voluntarily imposed privations on himself but rather see him at all times content and in good courage in every external circumstance; how in his vocational life and in outward relationships he always showed humility; and how, without either being ashamed of himself or placing any special merit on the matter, he candidly declared: "the Son of Man has nowhere to lay his head."[4] In exactly the same way we also find him here in his final suffering, enduring in patient calm when there was no help, and during which time he occupied himself with spiritual and divine matters in the inner depths of his heart and mind. But with regard to the suffering for which help was available, this is where we find him composed and calm and asking if by any chance he could receive help.

Moreover, we also see that during his public life and teaching by means of word and action how he had at all times testified to the fact that sinful human beings cannot make themselves pleasing to God or earn merit in heaven precisely by imposing privations on oneself and voluntarily seeking to take on oneself all kinds of suffering. Therefore he sought out those who labored and were heavily burdened—not only to revive them in body—but rather much more, namely, to set them spiritually free from the fruitless yet heavy yoke of such external works and from false confidence in them. We also see him now in his final suffering far from any such thoughts such as whether it was fitting for him to suffer more than he had to and thereby display an even greater strength of soul, and neither did he seek to increase the number of times he had to exercise self-control, and so prove himself to be virtuous. On the contrary, from anything that was painful that he could blamelessly divert from himself still even at this point he sought to free himself as much as he was able. Hence, when the roof of his mouth dried up and he called out, "I thirst," he thereby clearly demonstrates to us that he had no wish to boast of any other strength of spirit than that of a genuine obedience that not only acts but also endures all the unavoidable things that happen and that are to be borne by every person in one's position in human society in the most faithful fulfillment of the divine will. Moreover, only in the strength of this pure and steadfast obedience was his death agony in the spiritual sense the great turning point at which a former way of life came to an end. That was a way of life that involved not only the

4. Eds.—Matt 8:20b.

illusion of empty works but to a similar extent also the slavery to sin, and now that all hostile powers that opposed the salvation of human beings were defeated, a new life began.

Hence, as newly apprised of this example of our Redeemer and by means of it let us also not permit any thoughts to arise in us that still belong to that former way of life. Viewed from a physical perspective, our earthly life also cannot be anything other than a mixture of joy and pain. But as we consider the person who balances this mixture too precisely, and who when he is permitted to perform his proposed work without any great inconvenience thereupon pursues too anxiously every little comfort as if to have something good for the uncertain future—as I say, when we consider such an individual we have no special esteem for such a person. This is so, because his soul busies itself too earnestly with a trifling earthly settling of accounts so that we can only also feel sorry for him as a person who tortures himself. In times of misfortune he is as someone who cannot have enough misery, as one who in the normal course of life holds up every little hurt so that he can adorn himself with it, and also as one who disdains and rejects the relief from human beings which could be of help to him. In such a case as this, the act of disdaining any gift from above, even one more modest—and the sympathetic help of human beings is always such a gift—can never make us worthy in the sight of God.

But here there belongs yet another matter that we must not overlook before we move on to the second part of our reflections. Inasmuch as John says, "When Jesus knew that all was now finished, he said (in order to fulfill the scripture) 'I thirst,'" John wants to draw our attention to the fact that in that Psalm—as we know from our earlier reflections—that in these hours, there is a passage that was particularly on Christ's mind, which among other similarities expressed this aspect of his physical sufferings, namely, in that there it is stated, "My mouth is dried up like a potsherd, and my tongue sticks to my jaws."[5] Now, although the fact that in that psalm nothing is stated about any alleviation of this suffering, and the Redeemer's attention continued to be focused on the fact that those similarities to him and to his situation were in the process of being fulfilled, this, nevertheless, did not move him to reject the possibility of its being relieved.

Hence, the thought that it belonged to his destiny that this part of Scripture would also be fulfilled in him must not have had such an influence on him that he adjusted his behavior in accordance with it. Rather than this,

---

5. Ps 22:15.

he did not allow himself to be prevented from doing everything in relation to his suffering that he also would have done if this passage of Scripture had not at all been available. And we can also certainly believe that just as he had quenched his thirst, if he could have been of help to those who saw him, mocked him, and shook their heads, he whose hands were now pierced and whose bones could all be counted, those who gazed upon him, those who took pleasure in his condition, these persons he would also have readily set free. Thus, the directions about what he should do and what he should leave undone he derived not from the prophetic intimations of Scripture but from its commandments inasmuch as he applied them in their full power to himself. "In the scroll of the book it is written of me. I delight to do your will, O my God, your law is within my heart."[6]

This also, my good friends, is a salutary sign to us at a time when many Christians do not properly distinguish the one from the other, and, led by a well-intentioned but misplaced zeal for the truth of Scripture, apply themselves to the difficult business of investigating the hidden meaning of prophecies in such a way that as soon as they imagine a certainty where a hint exists, they not only rejoice about everything that seems to bring about its fulfillment, no matter how much a sound heart and mind would otherwise have to feel depressed, but also, in order to promote its fulfillment, they will unfortunately do certain things without asking whether such things are also in conformity with the will and law of God which they should bear in their hearts. Let all of us, then, guard ourselves against taking this wrong turning, and let us always distinguish what in Scripture is written for our instruction and discipline in righteousness, and what is set down for us only for our consideration whether as a story or as a prophecy.

II

The second matter that cannot be avoided in our reflections on this statement of Christ arises when we give proper attention to the circumstances in which the Redeemer found himself at that time. It is this, namely, that this very brief statement shows how free his heart was from any kind of defiance or resentment. This is so, for in view of the fact that he cried out, "I thirst," he must certainly have thought of the possibility that some help would be available to him, otherwise this statement of his, as brief as it certainly was, would have been as little heard as any futile complaint about what was

---

6. Ps 40:7b, 8.

inevitable. Now, who could render any assistance other than precisely the mercenaries who had kept watch beneath his cross? It was they who stood guard over him, and without their permission no one could approach his cross. But what could he otherwise see in these men if not in fact the same as in the similarly disposed associates of those who earlier let loose their shameful spite and wanton petulance on him? Who other than the most cruel servants of precisely the highest unlawful power under whose sway the Redeemer would not even normally want to live, and which now had pronounced his death sentence? Now, let us honestly ask ourselves, if we think of some other human heart, also pious and gentle only not yet wholly cleansed by the Holy Spirit but of such a heart from which all selfishness has been expelled and from which all pride has vanished. Would it not have been natural for such a person as this to prefer not to seek help from persons like those who were in circumstances of this kind and who themselves had even proved themselves to be of such a sort? Would this person not rather endure the many pains and torments that had to be borne in any case and also that of enduring a burning thirst specifically for the few moments that still remained of his earthly life than to call out for help to those who until now had done nothing other than scoff at the One who was suffering? My good friends, if we consider the words of the Redeemer from this perspective, then we will not even for one moment longer say that the request in and of itself is of no significance, but rather consider it to be of the utmost importance and to be set alongside that great statement which the Redeemer had made shortly before this, namely, "Father, forgive them, for they do not know what they are doing."[7]

For myself at least, it seems that we could put ourselves to the test with regard to this matter and in a similar situation ask which of the two would be easier: the first, with regard to the sense for law, in the consciousness that we have never deviated from a simple and blameless life before God, and that like the Lord throughout his entire life, so we have sought and willed nothing other than to fulfill the will of our heavenly Father; or also with this understanding, when our enemies encamp around us and mock us, to pray to the heavenly Father as Jesus did: "Father, forgive them for they do not know what they are doing."

Just as all of us have made the observation and also found it to be confirmed by repeated experiences that it is often easy enough for a person to endure more severe suffering in connection with which he can

7. Eds.—Luke 23:34a.

satisfactorily demonstrate his strength of soul, but that this same person who in such an exemplary way endured the greater suffering is often not in a position to overcome the lesser discomforts and adversities of life in the same way without ceasing in his customary mode of conduct or otherwise letting himself be overcome by them. This is so, but still I think it is also the same with the impulses of our hearts and minds in that where some matters of importance are concerned it is often easy to keep them under control and to let them be guided by the divine Spirit. Yet, precisely with regard to the details of life it is unexpectedly difficult and requires great efforts on such occasions to resist those matters in the human soul that are not wholly praiseworthy or without fault and that are nevertheless very naturally active in people's souls. Moreover, in any similar circumstance this is an experience that all of us will certainly have.

Now, if we ask the question as to the way we ourselves as well as the best people we know would probably have acted in this case if perhaps no involuntary expression of need had intervened—which with regard to the Redeemer cannot have happened—then we would have to admit that most likely in almost all of us the feeling that certainly would hold the upper hand would be that we would rather not want to accept any help and relief from those who already had so maliciously offended and insulted us. Yet, what else would this be other than a petty sentiment, one that might easily deteriorate into anger and enmity! Let us then suppose that the worst had happened, and that on the basis of this dispassionate statement of the Redeemer the mercenaries had again taken the opportunity to indulge in some sort of wanton mockery. Did the Redeemer incur some kind of disadvantage because of this? Would this have had the effect of casting a gloom over the peace of his soul? Or, after everything that had already happened must we not with the greatest certainty assume the opposite? Now, someone may respond as follows: the Redeemer would have admittedly, on this account as on all accounts, have been perfectly certain of himself, but we who are not able to answer for ourselves to the same degree would certainly do the wrong thing, and without even any anxiety we would abandon ourselves to the danger of needlessly losing our peace of mind—which is such a precious good in suffering—and this because of an offensive outburst against which we perhaps could not guard ourselves.

I too, my good friends, would indeed decide for this caution, when we are able to do it without offense to our duty. But take heed lest we do not have to think about this matter in this manner. God desires that all human beings should look on each other as brothers and sisters and love one another. For this reason he has arranged the world in such a way that no person lives for oneself alone but rather that each necessarily lives in community with many others and therefore, strictly speaking, indirectly with all. But this divine will that can, with such power, work its way through everything generated by divisiveness and disunity among human beings. It is first of all and in its entire extent and full power made known to us since that time when all of us received a common central focus in the Redeemer. This is so, for although Christians are still empowered and called to a special love of brothers and sisters among themselves, we indeed know most certainly—the power of redemption being universal—that between our brothers and sisters in Christ and those who are simply brothers and sisters in our common human frailty we make no other distinction than this, namely, that the former already participate in their salvation and that the others are nevertheless yet to attain it. But, as widely as the proper knowledge of this is also spread among us, all of us nonetheless still remain far behind in the fulfillment of this divine will, and in various ways we will still be tempted to be indifferent towards the former and to be averse towards the latter. Frequently this temptation comes to us precisely from our feeling for the beautiful and just and from our zeal for what is good and true. Hence, at every opportunity it is then the sacred duty of us all to revert to this consciousness of universal association and solidarity and firmly establish ourselves in this understanding. In this matter the heart becomes steadfast only with constant practice, and for this reason we should never ever deny this either to ourselves or to our siblings. Still, we can only practice this in part—principally only when we participate with such persons with whom we exist in no closer relationship whatever and render them assistance in matters common to all human beings. In part we can also do the same by means of letting them share in our lives and by seeking and accepting different forms of assistance from them.

However, there are cases when in some connection someone has shown him- or herself to be hostile towards us. Regarding this, I will not even consider how often we have falsely held this belief, as when a sense of harm caused by another person who bears us no ill will has sprung up within us. But it is certainly the case that there are persons who have deliberately vexed us and by means of repeated attacks exhausted us, and who in their being opposed to us have twisted and violated what is right. Yet on this account would we be entitled to withdraw our help if such persons should meet with any kind of misfortune? To do so would surely be to act in a very unchristian way, for such persons can never forfeit those claims on us that are based on the universal interconnection of human beings. Moreover, it is indeed also required of us to uproot as soon as possible the memory of such disturbances that only all too easily hurt us deeply and to maintain the relationship by which God himself has joined us together and not to let it be upset by false moves, however painful they may have been for us. For this reason we will grasp every opportunity to be of help to those who take themselves to be our enemies. This we will do as moved by a kind heart and by a proper love so that we can all the better preserve the equilibrium of our own souls, or give the same back to them in return for their help so that to the best of our abilities we may strengthen the divine law among all human beings.

All the same, should we here make a distinction between our certainly wanting to be of help to them and our not wanting to accept any help from them? Does this refusal to accept help not only mean that we adorn only ourselves with that which is easier and more pleasant and to impose on them what is more bitter and difficult? And it is truly certain that whoever will not accept help from the one who has insulted him will so much the less allow himself to please the one who has caused him the misfortune of being insulted.

Moreover, given this disposition, how indeed would any closer relationship be possible between hearts and minds that were at one time far estranged from one another? This is the case, since if relationality does not arise from the innermost heart of both parties on the basis of a human and of a Christian understanding, then indeed any other attempt will clearly either be ineffective or have merely an apparent and passing effect. Accordingly, just as it is a sacred duty to accept help from those who insult us, it is an equally sacred duty to provide help to them.

Take heed, then, how the Redeemer has led the way for us in regard to these two matters. Just as he healed the wounded ear of the servant of the high priest and thereby gave help to a person who when Christ was taken into custody must have actively conducted himself in a way that was thoroughly spiteful, here the Redeemer now cries out, "I thirst," and with the most friendly heart toward human beings holds out the opportunity to the Roman mercenaries who in their coarse wantonness had already exerted themselves to do him harm, an action that to some extent would conceal their enmity by means of a gesture of humane assistance that would enable them to be reconciled again with the world. O, what divine purity of soul the Redeemer demonstrates to us also in this action! How invincible was his disposition to embrace the entire human race with love, and how, under the most unfavorable circumstances. This love breaks through everything from the least to the greatest! In this matter may we seek to become like him, by overcoming all anger, and also in suffering by not letting ourselves grow to become hard of heart and obdurate, but rather seeking to let the entire fullness of love and its tender impartiality guard us even against our adversaries.

III

In closing there is still one further matter we must consider in connection with these words of the Redeemer, namely, whether for his own part he was ready not only to accept help from his adversaries and that for this reason addressed even them, but also that he did this in the good faith that the help he requested would not be forthcoming. So, according to this, just as little as we can believe that the utterance of the Redeemer was merely an involuntary cry having no particular purpose, just as little then can we think that he assumed that his request would be refused and that again they would take the opportunity to indulge in some renewed form of abuse. And in so doing, in this view, by his unruffled composure he really intended, on the one hand, to prepare himself for a victory, but on the other hand, to reveal those men in their total inhumanity if his suffering condition itself could not earn them any active sympathy and if their hostility would extend even to the smallest detail and be maintained even to the final moment. No! This we cannot believe with regard to our Redeemer. Hence, we have no other option than quite simply to accept the fact that when he called out, "I thirst," he did this on the basis of the human feeling that to the thirsty person there will also be given that which can quench his thirst. Indeed, he believed that the spiteful ill will that had been vented on him would now be seen to have been sated, and at the intensification of his suffering to death the original goodheartedness of human nature would again work its way through; hence it was for this reason that he called out, "I thirst."

Moreover, almost from the point at which the Redeemer stepped forth in public, how many, if not quite all, were the things that happened to him whereby this faith could have been weakened and uprooted! To a great extent his good deeds were received with indifference so that he cried woe to the towns where he had performed most of his symbolic acts and as a result had repeatedly experienced the apathy of human beings. With his life endangered there came to him the witness that he himself gave and which indeed in every moment was confirmed by his activity, and so he knew how badly things stood with the capacity of people to recognize his higher dignity. He knew how easy it was for crowds of people to be incited by those who persecuted him most. And even now he gave witness, after he discovered a traitor among the little band of his disciples, an event that brought about this decision about his earthly life whereby people of the most different kinds and also of opposing opinions and aspirations had banded against him; after they who had otherwise admired him with the same ardor now declared, "Crucify him"; after the authorities who should have protected him but who were now made cowardly by hostile insinuations delivered him up to death and surrendered him to the most malicious abuses; and after princely and aristocratic persons had testified to their pleasure in the base mockery that had been meted out to him and even the teachers of the people who stooped to taking pleasure in insulting him at the sight of his suffering unto death. What a wonder it would have been had there been no trace of belief in humanity found in him! Indeed, this would be a wonder regarding all others rather than regarding him!

This is so in him, for the more indissolubly the divine being was united with the human nature and wholly permeated it, the more it was also proper for him to believe that it could never be entirely separated from the relationship with the divine being, and also to believe that even in the most depraved people there still lay hidden something of the divine power of love, a divine love that will never fail in what is asked of it, so that at some point it would come to light. Despite the fact that so many different expressions of human depravity were concentrated against this person, who did not judge others, the truth could not in the least become clouded. Moreover, in that here too he was true to this faith with regard to the smallest of things inasmuch as he counted on the humanity of those who had already sufficiently demonstrated their inhumanity, he was also not disappointed. This is so, for one person from among the same mercenaries who had already cast lots for his garments, and perhaps also from among those who mocking him had clothed him in purple, now dipped a sponge in his own drink and reached it up to him on the cross. Hence, since he himself was free from all anger and all unbelief, by the power of love he defeated even those who had prepared for him the sufferings of death. Such is the case, in that for the final agony of his earthly life it was from them that he received relief, and we can say that with this brief statement, namely, "I thirst," expressing as it does his own reconciliation with his enemies and his faith in their receptivity for the good: that great saying, "Father, forgive them, for they do not know what they are doing," is now fully confirmed and sealed.

Hence, my good friends, also in this respect the Redeemer became for us a great and glorious example, certainly beyond our reach, yet whom we should indeed follow, recalling the saying that those who do not have the Spirit of Christ also do not belong to him. With this lively memory of this reconciling and deeply faithful word of the Redeemer, let us therefore guard ourselves all the more against everything that must necessarily upset us in this our discipleship. How, then, does it stand with us in this respect? All of us know very well that what I have just stated is the Redeemer's principle, namely, that all goodness can never entirely vanish from human nature for the reason that otherwise the capacity to accept him as the Redeemer would have to disappear. We also know just as well that indeed, even with regard to the matter of redemption, the growth of human beings in goodness can only be very slow. This is especially the case if they are to be certain of this. These are two matters of which we have an understanding, and certainly no one among us would ever express himself differently about this. Still, how imperfect things can be with regard to the liveliness of this knowledge and its application above all in the particularly troubled times of life! This is especially so when we are irritated by the common concerns of humanity, or when our own life has taken a questionable turn.

In our call let us allow something joyful to befall us through human interaction, even though we are more willing to attribute such movement of joy to more noble foundations that have, on that account, been effective. And so let us be willing to place human interaction on a higher level than we are wont to do. After having experienced a long period of conflict let us especially participate in some good thing as at the last and for once, encouraged and favored act, so that we immediately think that our eyes have now suddenly been opened and our hearts warmed and that this will now continue according to the same measure even though on occasions of calmer reflection we have often said to ourselves how impossible this is. But just as readily we will then also meet with the opposite. When people personally and passionately confront us and we are conscious of the fact that one should will only what is good, we think all too readily that it is enmity toward the good that engenders their hostility even though in calm circumstances we say often enough that carefully considered there is really no such thing as enmity to the good. The Redeemer did not encounter hostility against himself, but under the most unfavorable circumstances such as none of us can ever have got into, rather kept the good faith. Apart from his faith, truth and even redemption could also not have made progress, and the Reign of God would not have been established. Hence, let us by no means forget that in the same way he also kept himself free from enmity to the good.

In order that the example he gave on the cross not become lost to us, then in times of suffering and of disheartening circumstances affecting our neighbors—as well as in times of cheerfulness and of well-supported activity that promised positive outcomes—we have to direct ourselves to him. Above all, we have to guard ourselves against radically shifting our opinions of people in general and make the Redeemer's impartiality our own. If we want to receive the freedom of the Spirit, this is the first condition that belongs so essentially to the freedom of God's children. And if there are times in the important affairs of human beings when it seems as though a hostile and selfish spirit retains the upper hand, and that also among Christians the feeling of familial love and interconnectedness is diminishing and that we want to be gain victory over this, then indeed beforehand we also have to practice delight in small things when the great things do not delight us. Moreover, as the Redeemer did here, we have to learn to be satisfied when from a puffed up chest we are able to evoke only a few traces of human feeling. This first condition of evil—also present in the most offensive form of enmity—is not to become capable of overcoming the good that is in us, namely, the reconciling steadfastness and the gentle complaisance of love. This is also what we have to learn from him.

Therefore, as it has also appeared to us here, may his fair image frequently occupy our minds, and may we indeed look often to this calm inner freedom and this purity of soul in which even the slightest small cloud of ill-will never arose to cloud not only his imperishable communion with the Father, who is love, but also with the human race, which is the object of this love! To this end may it be that we ever more be formed according to the features of this image, and up to the last moments of our lives may we persevere in his likeness, and as also appearing here in this form, may these reflections on his suffering be a blessing to all of us. Amen.

6

The Last Look on Life

Passion Sermon, April 15, 1821[1]

Text: John 19:30a

When Jesus had received the wine, he said, "It is finished."

My devout friends, the most important and most glorious statement from among our Redeemer's last words from the cross is directly connected with the one that seems to be the least important and most trifling. The Lord called out, "I am thirsty."[2] Then the moistened sponge was offered to him, and when he had taken the unpleasant yet soothing drink he said, "It is finished." In addition to this, we should not disturb the connection between these statements because the apostle has linked them most closely together precisely in this way in that prior to this reporting that he says: "when Jesus knew that all was now finished, he said (in order to fulfill scripture) . . ."[3] And just as this first statement is the least significant among these last words of the Redeemer, since in itself its subject deals simply with the relief of a physical need, the second is indeed without question the most important among the last words of the Redeemer. This is the word that almost always has been the anchor for the faith of

---

1. Eds.—This sermon was preached in Holy Trinity Church, Berlin on Palm Sunday, April 15, 1821. The textual basis for the translation is SW II.2 (1843) 138–50. This sermon is also available in KGA III.2, 135–46.

2. Eds.—John 19:28.

3. Eds.—John 19:28a.

Christians, the word in which this faith has been fully confirmed and glorified, namely, that in accordance with the divine counsel the salvation of human beings can be gained in no other way than through him who was sent into the world for their salvation and who had to be obedient to death on the cross. But if our attention is directed solely to this important word, the immensity of the subject overwhelms us, hence we have to be glad that the apostle himself who has preserved this word for us has also left for us a key to it that gives our reflections a more specific direction. We find this very key in those preceding words, namely, "when Jesus knew that all was now finished, he said (in order to fulfill scripture), 'I thirst.'" In this parallel everything that had happened to him up to this point was in accordance with the divine promises as they had been expressed in the entire range of revelations as recounted in the written Word of God. John knew that in his soul the Redeemer was occupied with this parallel, and since he held promise and fulfilment over against one another in his human consciousness and knew that the divine decree was to be fulfilled in this in this way, he exclaimed, "It is finished."

In that moment everything was certainly not finished. Just as our redemption from sin is interconnected with our justification before God, in the same way the One who had to die for our sin also had to be raised for our justification.[4] In the same way this is also interrelated with the fact that his disciples saw the Father only in him, and that he, when he again departed the world, also again returned to the Father. Moreover, in the same way this is also related to the fact that he loved his own, and that he could not leave them orphaned but had to send them another Advocate who would remain with them and after them also with us, namely, the Spirit of truth. But the spiritual eye of the Redeemer saw all things as being finished in the sacred moment of his death, and it is precisely for this reason that this is also for us the central focus of our faith. This is so, for it was by being obedient unto death that he gained for us the life-giving Spirit, and accordingly, that having suffered, he has been crowned with glory and honor. Hence, if in the moment of his death he could in this sense say "it is finished," he must be reflecting on his death in the context of this limitless interconnection, which begins with the first promise that was given to fallen human beings about the seed of the woman and that extends forward to that endlessness when he will also bring to the Father all those whom the Father had given

---

4. Eds.—Rom 4:25.

him so that they will share in the praise and in the glory with which he had been crowned. Now certainly this is also completely true.

However, our intention is to return to that more specific direction which the apostle points out to us and to limit ourselves to some reflections on this word as being truly the final look on the life that he has laid aside. First of all, specifically, we will consider how during the course of his earthly life the Redeemer acknowledged the fulfillment of his destiny in this event. But then secondly, as our heart urges us to do so, we will consider how this important word of the Lord can also be applied to ourselves.

I

My good friends, just as the Redeemer said so often during his earthly life that he does nothing of himself but does only what he sees the Father doing, and that he says only what he has heard from the Father, we therefore find it natural that in his being exalted above every human frailty of spirit, still even now in these final agonizing hours of life, he was constantly engaged in the most deeply inward reflections on the ways of God. In this respect all the statements in the old covenant about the divine revelations that related to him were present in his soul. We have also already seen an example of this in his earlier words from the cross, and how also the pains and insults that he had to endure called to mind for him statements from Holy Scripture from among which he applied this one and that one to his condition. But, my good friends, we would certainly misunderstand him if we were to believe that it was in these details that he discovered that all things were finished in order that Scripture would be fulfilled. The fact was that he hung there on the cross surrounded by powerful enemies who had brought about his death, that his body pined away and his tongue stuck to the roof of his mouth, that he saw how his clothing was divided by the mercenaries and that lots were cast for his robe. Reflecting on such individual circumstances and comparing them with the words of the psalm could to a certain extent have diverted the attention of the suffering Redeemer from the tormenting feeling of physical pain—and indeed more so than would have been the case with for any other person. But these external circumstances could not completely occupy his soul, which was always directed towards greater things, and it was not because of these that with such a sense of relief he called out, "It is finished."

If we are to look for some matter of more importance then indeed we shall not want to let our own thoughts do as they please, for they certainly would not reach to Christ. Rather than this we should think of such statements of Scripture which his disciples apply to him when they speak with enthusiastic agreement about the essential things in his life and which here most naturally must also appeared before him. Where, then, are we to find his entire vocation to a fallen and sick human race more fully expressed than first of all in those words of the prophets in which one of the evangelists describes the entire mode of conduct of the Redeemer? Here I have in mind the gentle yet ever so powerful statements such as, "He will not break a bruised reed or quench a smoldering wick."[5] These are words that he had acted on throughout his entire vocational life up to this point, and which he enacted now in that he died, words that reached their fulfillment for the whole human race, which indeed could only be regarded as a bruised reed and a smoldering candle. Hence, even now, in the midst of death and confronting death alone, he could certainly feel himself called upon, together with the one from whom he had borrowed the words, "My God, my God, why have you forsaken me?"[6] to praise and glorify the name of his Father in a great congregation. Therefore, he also found that other statement wholly fulfilled, one which his disciples had at all times applied to him, namely, that he bore our sickness and that by his suffering we are healed,[7] and it was this that with the last look on his life he now saw finished so that Scripture would be fulfilled.

Still, my good friends, we can truly feel the full importance of this last word of Christ only if we first know how to put ourselves in the place of all those who with a still weak and imperfect faith attached themselves to the Lord at that time and do so in that frame of mind. When he entered the capital city of his people to be present at the feast which became the feast of his death and resurrection, and there was hailed by thousands as the One who is to come in the name of the Lord as the promised son of David, and when the palms were strewn at his feet—the sign of those who were victorious, and with their victory also the sign of the ruler who brings peace—what were the expectations undoubtedly alive at that time in the hearts and minds of this crowd which was drunk with joy and which flocked around him from all directions so that they could participate in the

---

5. Eds.—Isa 42:3; Matt 12:20.
6. Eds.—Ps 22:1 and Matt 27:46.
7. Eds.—See 1 Pet 2:24.

glorious entry? Unfortunately, these were expectations of an external glory and power such as the Redeemer had never encouraged, and which he had not come to fulfill. And there were also disciples of his who shared such a view, even though many sayings must have been alive in their memories by means of which at every opportunity the Redeemer frequently diverted their hopes and their love away from the glory of this earth and had pointed them to the spiritual world to which he as their Lord and master would be subject. They too were still not yet certain as to whether or not even at a later time in some way some external power and might would also become the means toward establishing this Reign of the Spirit in its full splendor so that perhaps they also, on account of these voices of the people, would be made drunk along with them by such earthly expectations in those glorious days. But the palm branches that on this occasion were strewn at the Redeemer's feet were now woven into the glorious crown of victory on the head of the dying Lord. Indeed, everything that was said then, arising as it did from human misunderstanding, now reached fulfillment in its true spiritual sense in accordance with the hidden divine decree. Hence, dying on the cross in this way Christ was truly the One who was to come in the name of the Lord, and for this reason and no other he is to be praised in the highest from that moment on into eternity.

The disciple who recorded this saying for us also felt it in this way, and it is for this reason that he says, "When Jesus knew that all was now finished . . . in order to fulfill scripture" so that Scripture had now been completely fulfilled in him, and that however much the great crowd had all along been wrong in their interpretation of all these glorious statements of the prophets, their true content would now be better understood by everyone so that also in this sense everything was finished in order that Scripture would be fulfilled. Here he proclaims it, this great statement of his own witness to himself, and here he does this so emphatically in order to recall his disciples forever from every false earthly expectation. Hence, it was for this reason that he proclaimed, "It is finished!" Moreover, now they knew that like their Lord and Master they also would fare no better than he; that they would fulfill their calling in no other way than through suffering and affliction and thereby be enabled to enter into the Reign of his glory. Now they knew that "flesh and blood cannot inherit the reign of God,"[8] because the flesh and blood of Christ had nailed hope in flesh and blood to the cross. Therefore that they also should now "regard no

---

8. Eds.—1 Cor 15:50a.

one from a human point of view."⁹ Now they knew that his entire work was purely spiritual, and that his power for which they strive and which they are to spread abroad is none other than that of the Lord, who as the Crucified One builds it up in the hearts of human beings.

However, my good friends, there is still another matter that we should not overlook inasmuch as in this connection with the fulfillment of Scripture the Redeemer bursts out, "It is finished." No, we surely have to sense that it is not solely—indeed not even primarily—a question of his activity that he looks back on and regard this as his own work. But rather, and above all, he points to what happened to him and through him. The fact that he reached this goal of his great destiny at such an early age was not his own work, and he could not have wanted to present it as such in these words. On the contrary, it was the fulfillment of the divine decree by means of divine guidance and divine providence. His death was the great moment to which all things human had to work together from the very first beginning of our race. It had been hinted at long before in the various images of the suffering of God's servants in a perverse world. Moreover, who would want to deny that these images, wherever they are to be found, were in fact expressions from above of an enlightened consciousness even though in the form of a weak reflection. Nevertheless, these images became ever clearer as they became more prominent in the discourses of these godly men who were filled with the divine Spirit. Now they were fulfilled because the appearance of the Redeemer was a scandal and a folly to the perversity of the human heart, and because such perversity grew and increased to become malice and spite precisely on account of the faith in and love toward the Redeemer that had begun to develop. This was what happened to him, and this above all was what he now beheld. He had already completed his active life with that glorious prayer which the same Gospel writer has preserved¹⁰ in which he gave an account to his Father of how the Father had glorified him throughout the course of his entire life, and in which at the same time he also expressed the hope that the Father will now glorify the Son. He was so confident in this and so fully conscious of the duty now completely and genuinely fulfilled that at that time he also appeared before God with those whom the Father had given him and chosen from the world. Yet, at that time he certainly did not express these great words, "It is finished." But

---

9. Eds.—2 Cor 5:16a.

10. John 17. Eds.—This is our translation of Schleiermacher who is not directly quoting the biblical text.

if in fact since that point he had in the proper sense done nothing further, to what are we referred that explains how it was only now that he could say, "It is finished," and not yet at that time before this? It is indicated very clearly in this, my good friends, namely, that the divine decree with regard to human beings is never fulfilled only by means of what human beings do, and for him also, the only One in grace, for the only righteous One this also held good. The divine decree is always fulfilled only by means of the working together of every power that the Highest puts into action—not only of those of whom in a narrower sense we can say he grants the will and the fulfillment, but also of those of whom we most favorably think that God simply speaks to them and says, "this far and no further." The divine decree is fulfilled by means of the deeply hidden interlocking of all times and all space, and one day must tell it to another, the earth tell it to heaven and again heaven to earth.[11] It is on account of all these things together and never on the basis of that which the individual human being alone is capable of and accomplishes that one can say, "It is finished."

Hence, my good friends, this word of the Lord demonstrates to us that in his final great moments he forgot or placed in the background even his own activities on earth, which he had just concluded, in order to direct his final observation once again solely to the deeds of his Father. What was fulfilled in the final moment of his earthly existence was this, namely, that he immersed himself in the mystery of the divine decrees. Therefore even in this great moment of his passing, as much as in another way, it was also his own action and his most sacred merit that was fulfilled. This fulfillment was rather one that he most preferred to regard, not only as announced in advance, but also as prepared in advance, and as one that was now directly accomplished only by means of the interrelated and interactive purposes of the divine wisdom.

II

Now, if this is the right understanding of the attitude of heart and mind in which the Redeemer uttered the words of our text, in the greatest and most important words from among those of his final statements we also discern the most profound humility of the One "who, though he was in the form of God, did not regard equality with God as something to be exploited,"[12] but

11. Eds.—See Ps 19:1–4.
12. Eds.—Phil 2:6–7.

placing his own work and merit in the shadow of the final moments of his life, he satisfies himself by rejoicing only in the fact that the decree of his Father has reached its fulfillment. How, then, can we apply these words to ourselves? And how should I respond to the statement I have made regarding this second part of our reflections? Indeed, if here it is a matter of the active life, of the human agency of the Redeemer, would we also not then of course have to ask, what indeed are we compared with him? And could any person among us have a mind to compare oneself with him? Nevertheless, in this regard, its application to us may well go better all the same. This is so, for when Christ concluded his account with his heavenly Father in that high-priestly prayer which I have already mentioned, his situation then was exactly the same as it is with other human beings. Although God was in him and reconciled the world to himself through him,[13] nevertheless, the world that he beheld was one that was still unreconciled and surrounded by darkness and the shadow of death. Moreover, he presented to his Father as the fruit of his life only the very few who had committed themselves to him in faith and love as those who were now chosen from the world so that with a joyful heart he could say, "They do not belong to the world, just as I do not belong to the world . . . they have received the words (you gave to me) and know that I come from you."[14] Here he also had to mourn a lost sheep so that in his immediate circle what he himself had said would be fulfilled, namely, that "many are called, but few are chosen,[15] and so that he too would learn that with regard to the matter of having an effect on human beings there is no complete success without failure. Here also he had to come before his heavenly Father with prayers for the work to which from a human point of view he was to remove his hands. Moreover, in this way he thereby confessed that although in a different and higher sense he had accomplished everything, nevertheless, only now had he just begun the process of bringing it to its final outcome and that the Father alone would have to complete what the Son could only initiate.

Here, my good friends, when it is a matter of the soul's final address to God, we can surely find many things that we can apply to ourselves before we depart this world. All of us have those whom the Lord has given us so that we can present them as chosen from the world. Moreover, any person who has faithfully and sincerely promoted the work of the Lord on

---

13. Eds.—See 2 Cor 5:19a.
14. Eds.—John 17:16; 17:8.
15. Eds.—Matt 20:16.

earth even though with a feeling of one's own weakness and has wanted to do nothing other than this, will also be able devoutly to say, "Here am I, Father, together with those you have given me." Moreover, whoever, like the Redeemer, has to heave a sigh over disappointed hopes, when also this person or that has vigorously torn oneself away from the loving and guiding hand in spite of all supportive and sustaining love, this person too, like the One who suffered so that Scripture would be fulfilled, will then also not be denied a comfort.

Still, this is not exactly what this important word of the Redeemer is about. Rather, it concerns that which happened to him so that all Scripture would be fulfilled concerning him without anything being left unfulfilled. Now, what kind of comparison can we make here? As he himself says, Scripture bears witness to him on every page. This is so, when the Spirit of God enlightens the eye of the reader, when Scripture presents him as its promised One from the very beginning and sets him before our eyes as the One in whom it is fulfilled in the words, "It is finished," does it also speak about us, my good friends? Can we also cast such a look to the past at the end of our lives so that we can rejoice in the fact that Scripture is fulfilled in us? Oh, yes, it certainly is; it speaks about all of us! Does it not say that all of us are sinners and that we lack the reputation with God which we are supposed to have?[16] You see, this is the first statement of Scripture that is fulfilled in all of us. And in the last moments of our lives, when we reflect, and our eyes are directed to times now past, and above all to the One in whom the glory of God and the divine will is demonstrated for all of us—ah! then indeed everyone will say, now that I am dying, this text of Scripture is finally fulfilled in me! But Scripture also states, "Christ Jesus who became for us wisdom from God, and righteousness and sanctification and redemption."[17] Now then! Whoever has to boast of God's grace, whoever has not become deaf to the voice of his Spirit, whoever finds himself or herself in living communion with Christ in whom the two groups are made one,[18] and who in the final moments can look back on such a life that has been lived by faith in the Son of God and by Christ's life in him or her, for such a person these texts of Scripture are the most authentic expression of the consciousness that defines the full and complete content of his life. But, what is not to be brought under this heading is that which also does

16. Eds.—See Rom 3:23.
17. Eds.—1 Cor 1:30.
18. Eds.—Eph 2:14.

not belong to the content of his life. And in this faithful feeling that this Scripture, which edifies and blesses, has also been fulfilled in her or him so that she or he can confess "it is finished."

Nevertheless, my good friends, let us not leave the matter at the most general aspects of our faith and stop at the consciousness of blessedness which is found in communion with the Redeemer. But rather, and of course always only through him and with him, in this way and in communion with the Redeemer, we can nevertheless certainly also still continue to pursue further the similarity between these words from his mouth and the moment of our own departure, or rather, our last look on our past life, with as complete a consciousness as yet to be granted to us as that which was granted to the Redeemer. This is so, my good friends, because the full appearance of the Redeemer, but most particularly the great moment in which he as dying accomplished the work of reconciling the world to God, was to such an extent as no other the great turning point at which two different eras were separated from one another, namely, that of blessed fulfillment and that of the faith that is active in the love that is creative and life-giving. But all of us together, and of course each one of us also, however weak and insignificant our existence in the world may be, are in fact in a similar way also taken up into the great mutually interacting connections of the ways in which God leads us. This is so, for it is indeed the case that the same things recur in the Lord's church again and again only to a lesser degree. As Christ spoke to his disciples telling them that he still had many things to say to them but that they could not bear them now,[19] and then referred them to the Spirit, whom he would send to them, he at that point also established for them a new time of longing and expectation that would reach fulfillment only later. Moreover, everything that we still recognize in the present as a deficiency and as an imperfection arouses such longing and expectation in us. Fulfillment comes later. But this imperfection only endures so long—even if we are not able to quit longing and hoping—that is until that time at which the age of the perfection of the humanity of Christ is attained when we find that all things are so arranged that longing and fulfillment alternate with each other. But now it is the case that as soon as one thing is fulfilled—even though only incompletely—we already long for another. But to this unfinished fulfillment something that belongs to the well-pleasing will of God should be brought by each living generation. Thereby all that remains to be fulfilled is what is left to the next generations.

19. Eds.—John 16:12.

Moreover, every person who as a living member of this body sanctified by God is also to be praised when to this work of his contemporaries he makes his own contribution, as one should. But just as in fact not everything that was to happen had already taken place when the Redeemer declared, "It is finished," so we also, in the same faith with which we behold "the pioneer and perfecter of our faith,"[20] can nevertheless regard that which still lies ahead of us as comprised in that which has already ensued. And it is exactly the same with regard to the last look on the life, brought to completion as with inward gratitude to God, we remain dependent not upon that achieved by means of our own merit. For this matter has to do solely with the Lord, and also not upon our autonomous action, for our external situation, and indeed many things that do not depend on us, also always work together in connection with this matter. But rather, it is most certainly brought to some completion as mediated by our presence, our actions, and our various indirect influences, or through the presentiment that the line that marks at least the beginning of fulfillment has been crossed.

Moreover, on account of the singularity of our existence as well as the circumstances in which God has placed us, we should embrace this as that which is promised to us. And we should certainly value this, and at the moment of the last look on life humbly and thankfully praise God for the fact that what he has assigned to us by his wisdom as our daily task is also now truly finished. With humility we will recognize how much had to come to us from without in order to be useful to us. In this way even only the little that happens really happens through us when the circumstances are favorable or through assistance from outside so that we search everywhere in vain for any work that is exclusively ours. But then, God willing, we will also be thankful to have recognized everything with regard to how indeed even in us, if only to a slight degree, the excellent words of Scripture are fulfilled, namely, that all the gifts of the Spirit are manifested for the common good.[21] And we will also recognize that when Scripture presents the gifts of the Spirit together in their refreshing variety as "love, joy, peace, patience, kindness, generosity, faithfulness, gentleness and self-control,"[22] some of these, even if they were not fully matured and of the most sought after beauty, have indeed also grown in the garden of our hearts and minds.

20. Eds.—Heb 12:2a.
21. 1 Cor 12:7. Eds.—This is our translation of Schleiermacher, who is not directly quoting the biblical text.
22. Gal 5:22.

Indeed, Christ alone was the one human being in whom everything that properly belonged to the image of God in this human nature always grew undisturbed and developed in the finest proportions. Moreover, the time in which he appeared and the circumstances under which he lived contributed nothing to this but only to the fact that this glory of the only begotten Son could only be active according to the way and the measure of how the divine wisdom had decided from eternity. And this he also found to be finished when still on the cross this glory appeared in a most wondrous way in its full splendor. With us this is certainly different, and no one can look back on one's life without observing the changing and unsteady movement of one's soul. Falling and rising again, putting one's hand to the plough and then again looking back in doubt, readily undertaking God's work and then again loosening one's grasp in discouragement, this and no other is the way of our spiritual life, only differently shaped in the bloom of youth, different in its gradual maturing, and different in each person according to the measure of one's particular nature and one's external circumstances. But no matter how distressing this may be from a different point of view, if we, like Christ, at the end of our life only regard it less on the basis of what we ourselves have done and much rather on the basis of what God has done through us and for us according to his gracious decree and preparation then in this respect we will also be like him for at our life's end everything will coincide in a joyful "It is finished." Then the divine Word is held up to us as a clear mirror of truth. Each of us can recognize ourselves in this. If we have really looked at it closely then we are obligated to bear witness—even though we have once or perhaps more frequently forgotten—to the way we have been formed. We have repeatedly been led back to it to look into it anew, and even our hesitations and failures, our negligence and our harmful desires have had to develop in such a way as to bring us to a greater depth and clarity in our knowledge of ourselves. To depart this life with such knowledge as this is among the greatest of goods that can be granted to us. If once we have been turned away from the great universal confusion of the human race to the true shepherd and guardian of our souls and have discovered that it is with him that we find peace and quickening; if once we have then also searched for another protection that seemed to be closer at hand to us after having experienced the despair of the human heart when some difficult matter has posed a threat to us; or when after the heart's stubbornness we dared to enter alone into pastures that mislead us, even then he has nevertheless pursued us in different ways, and because of these unrelated experiences we have become all the more convinced that protection and certainty as well as well-being and quickening are to be found only in relation to him. If indeed under the world's pressure and obduracy we have repeatedly formed the impression that the Lord with whose talent we are entrusted and on which we are to get a good return is a harsh man who would want to reap where he has not sown,[23] then indeed we would—now in one way, now in another—be prevented from burying it completely and would have to be shown what has been done with it, however little it may be. Therefore, when by means of God's gracious guidance, which also glorifies those whom he has justified,[24] God has also blotted out our weaknesses and aberrations not only for the sake of our being strengthened but also—for certainly we often experience this influence on account of the weaknesses of others—for that of our brothers and sisters who have served in the interest of instruction and warning and for correction in godliness. Then we shall have to confess that however true it remains with regard to that other text of Scripture, which all of us will apply to ourselves (each considered according to oneself because of the glory we are to have with God), this text too actually applies to every individual member of Christ's community as well as to the whole in which we are incorporated in connection with our common life of both suffering and action. This is the community in which the Word of Scripture has also been fulfilled and will be fulfilled ever anew so that for those who love God all things have to work together for good.[25]

If in this way, at some time in the future, we look back on the completed life from its goal, then we will thankfully and joyfully acknowledge the eternal and wise good and the merciful love of the heavenly Father for everyone who knows what it means to have been a child, who through errors and weaknesses, who through joy and suffering have united us ever more carefully, and finally inseparably with the One whom we dare not abandon if the Scripture is to be fulfilled in us, and in communion with whom we also, like him, will confidently declare, "It is finished." Amen.

---

23. Eds.—Matt 25:24.

24. Rom 8:30. Eds.—This is our translation of Schleiermacher, who is not directly quoting the biblical text.

25. Rom 8:28. Eds.—This is our translation of Schleiermacher, who is not directly quoting the biblical text.

7

Christ's Last Words to His Heavenly Father

Good Friday, April 20, 1824[1]

Text: Luke 23:46

Then Jesus, crying with a loud voice, said, "Father, into your hands I commend my spirit." Having said this, he breathed his last.

Prayer: Praise and honor to our Lord, who was obedient to death, to the end that he has given his life in death and bore many sins, that a great company should receive, gain, and plunder the powers. Amen

My devout friends, the first two Gospel writers tell us only that Jesus gave a loud cry,[2] and then died, but they do not report to us the last words that he spoke. John, who stood close to his cross, was so fully occupied with the words that were the subject of our recent reflections, and these important words, namely, "It is finished," had filled the ears of his spirit to such an extent that he did not record these calmer words of the Redeemer

---

1. Eds.—This sermon was preached in Holy Trinity Church, Berlin on Good Friday, April 20, 1821, in the afternoon. The textual basis for the translation is SW II.2 (1843) 151–60. This sermon is also available in KGA III.2, 147–55.

2. Eds.—Matt 27:50; Mark 15:37.

of which he was not aware and that perhaps were spoken later. Therefore, we are thankful for the knowledge that Luke, from whose account our text is taken, has preserved this word for us. Moreover, after those great words, namely, "It is finished," it is certain that all of us will pay no less attention to those recorded by Luke, but rather that for this solemn festival of our Lord's death and for this its sacred hour we acknowledge them to be a worthy subject for all of us to direct our devout reflections.

This is the last calm word from his soul addressed to his heavenly Father. On this understanding, my good friends, we will focus our attention first of all on portraying what [claim] this word in and of itself has to make on everyone who ponders it in his heart. Then secondly, in order for us better and more fully to understand it as the last word of our Redeemer, we will look back from this one to his earlier words from the cross and bring it into relation with these.

I

The Lord said: "Father, into your hands I commend my spirit." This, it may be added, is certainly a fully human word of our Lord, one that for this reason all of us can also wholly and completely appropriate for ourselves. Now, if for a moment we would be inclined to think that at any time in the life of the Redeemer the human and the divine in his person as distinct from each other were capable of doing this or that, everyone would of course say that at least these words could certainly not have proceeded solely from that which was God in him. The eternal Word was not a Word for itself alone, since, in fact, this Word became flesh and lived among us. Certainly, it could never stop being with God, as it had been by him from the beginning. Therefore it is not the case that this eternal Word for its own sake was only able to entrust himself to the Father of the Redeemer, but rather it was to the human soul alone, to that of Jesus in whom the Word became flesh and dwelled. Therefore, in these words of our Lord no special and somewhat concealed information grounded in the divine that dwelt in him is disclosed about what it is that awaits human beings when body and soul are separated from one another. Therefore, it is rather the case that the divine Word speaks here entirely in accordance with his human nature, which is the same as our own.

Just as little do these words sound like those of such a One who has mastery over death, and who on his own account has a certainty and confidence about it that no other person could have. Rather, what we listen to here is the wholly trusting surrender of a dying man who makes known the way in which every other pious person surrenders and commends himself to the divine omnipotence in the final moment of this life. Of course, my good friends, it is simply this same omnipotence that guards and upholds human beings during the earthly life. And what is seen to be true from one certain point of view is but in fact false and in error from another. Consider the desire to maintain in general and without qualification that the human, so long as he or she lives through him- or herself, is, here on earth, responsible for his or her own soul; and even if the individual is not responsible for the self alone, then humankind in community alone is able to help the individual. Nevertheless, we certainly feel very differently with regard to the transition from one moment of the earthly life to another. This is so inasmuch as we are and remain in possession of all the powers and means through which our own existence is supported along with the existence of the rest of the world and through which the world has an effect on us and we in turn react to it. And certainly, during this earthly life we feel different than we feel in the context of the mysterious workings of the divine omnipotence at the transition from the final moment of this earthly life to that which succeeds it. Now when all the bonds that unify the spirit with the rest of the world by means of the body are dissolved, and when these very means disappears at the same time at the last moment, then the next eternal moment not only holds the spirit fast and is at work in it, but we are also even allowed in the spirit to look across the divide of death, which is not allowed to humans in their own capacity, at least not with any certainty. Indeed, we might all the more feel that we would have become lost and gone completely astray outside the interrelationships of existence if the divine omnipotence had not taken initiatives to take hold of us and lead us across the valley of death.

But from the choice of his last words, "Father, into your hands I commend my spirit!" we readily understand that the Redeemer was endowed with such confidence that he could now regard what now lay before him as though it was no more significant than that which is precisely always the case with regard to the transition of one moment of human life to another. This is so, inasmuch as these words did not come exclusively from his own inner being and only for this moment, for they are also words from the Psalms as indeed are those earlier words from the cross that were derived from this book, namely, "My God, my God, why have

CHRIST'S LAST WORDS TO HIS HEAVENLY FATHER

you forsaken me."[3] They are the words of a pious man who is in no respect preoccupied with his departure from this world but rather is a person who still has much to expect and to request from God, the Lord of life, precisely with reference to the future course of this earthly life. They are the words of such a person who, in that he certainly has reason ardently to give thanks to God for the help God has granted him, nevertheless faces a future that is still filled with danger such that he bursts out with these words, "into your hands I commend my spirit. You, the true God have redeemed me."[4] And precisely these words of a person who is still involved with and in the midst of human life, yet who knows that everything he receives from it among the various dangers that threaten it, can come only from the hand of the same Lord who as present in every moment of his existence has ordered all things in accordance with his goodwill. These are the words of such a person that our Redeemer makes use of at the point of his complete departure from this world.

Does this not most certainly imply that the Redeemer found no significant difference between the one and the other? Here in the earthly life, the breath of life, the soul of the human being, is placed in the hand of the Lord. What will develop from every person and how it will develop is grounded in his order, and it can only go well with a person when he is commended to this ordering Lord and when in every moment he commends himself to him in each moment. But this is equally the mind of the Redeemer: that even at life's end there is to be found in the same hand that which should develop out of this end and which is ordered according to the same laws. Hence, here also, from the same surrender and commendation there arose for him the same joy. Moreover, it was this same disposition as that which here constantly leads us through all things that guided him across. If this seems to you to be too much, simply consider the fact that certainly not all of this comforting wisdom of the Lord is already found in those words which the Redeemer quotes here from the earlier and less perfect time of the old covenant. But there is one word, one that he adds, which is not at home in the Old Testament, namely, the great all-embracing word "Father." "Father," the Redeemer adds this of himself as his own. "Father, into your hands I commend my spirit." Hence, it is in this, my dear friends, that we are indeed to believe—that there is to be found the deepest foundation of this calm confidence in the certain consciousness of the Redeemer of his

---

3. Eds.—Ps 22:1 although Schleiermacher has cited Ps 31:6 in his footnote.
4. Eds.—Ps 31:5.

inward communion with the heavenly Father. Also in the moment of his death he feels himself to be the only and firstborn of the Father. It was from this source that amid all the circumstances of his life there came to him that unclouded equanimity of the disposition of his heart and mind, which is the unmistakable sign of the divinity of his being. Hence, at no moment was he restrained in any servile way out of fear of what could come, nor on account of an attractive and glittering prospect was he ever excited in any vain way. And this was because it was the divine in him that always called "Father," and because he always knew that he was one with the Father.

Moreover, if we then inquire about the ground of the consistent disposition and firm confidence in which the Redeemer now departed human life as moved in a way no different from how other pious persons are moved who revere the Lord take leave of one well-spent phase of life and go on to encounter a new significant moment, then we also should not seek further for something special, because the one right answer is to be found only in this word that he adds to those words of the psalm. He was the Son of the Father, and it was his communion with God that made it apparent to him that the transition from the earthly life to the state of exaltation was in no respect different from any transition that had already taken place in his life. This difference, which appears to all of us to be so great, paled for him entirely because the one is no more and no less than the other for the One in whom and with whom he alone lived—the One whose wisdom establishes the interconnection and order of all earthly things in accordance with his entire eternal reign.

Hence, just as at the point of his departure from this world, this firm confidence of the Redeemer was directly related to his being so completely immersed in the relationship to his Father that the sight of death could as little separate him from this relationship as could anything else in the midst of these earthly things; let us then for our own comfort not forget that the Redeemer consecrates us to this same communion with the Father. Moreover, it is only because of this that in this matter he can be our example so that we are capable of the same confidence, the confidence that has to be the particularly distinctive mark of the Christian. What a stage this represents! It ranges from the servile fear of death within those who look only into a darkness in which nothing of that appears which alone has lifted up their eyes from the obtuse indifference that is just as much rooted in the satiety of the consciousness set on the things of the flesh—as in the fretting of sensual powers—to the composed surrender of an earnest heart and mind in the face of an admittedly unknown but equally general as inevitable fate. But then yet further, it ranges to this confidence which rests on the relationship with God by virtue of the fact that the universal orderer and ruler of all things is not merely a being outside ourselves in whom we are to trust but rather the One who is in us and we in the One. Hence, on this account our will cannot be separated from God's nor God's from ours inasmuch as according to the great promise related to the new covenant, his law, and therefore also to the law of his Reign and ordering in creation, is written on our hearts in such a way that it can truly be said, as the Redeemer said it then, that the Father makes God's dwelling in our hearts. But, my good friends, to reach this point there is no other way, for Christ alone is the way;[5] and then as he also says, no one comes to the Father except through me.[6] But as he has promised, namely, that he will draw to himself those who believe in him when he will be exalted above the earth,[7] similarly he also draws his own to himself to this firm and inward confidence, and indeed what is more, to this complete oneness of will with the Father in which he was able to depart this earthly life. Moreover, he does this so that all of us, in the same measure as we are united with the Son, will also commit our spirits into God's hands with the same simple and childlike confidence, to the One for whom the living spirit cannot be lost, who as the One and eternal Lord and Preserver of all things is at the same time the true and trustworthy Father of everything it means to be a child.

II

This, my good friends, is therefore the both gentle and uplifting impression that the last word of the Redeemer—viewed in itself—must make upon us all. However, in order for us to understand it properly, let us now return from it to the earlier words of the Lord from the cross since nothing in his discourses, my good friends, stands by itself alone. Just as everything arose from the same source of his divine being, so all things are therefore one and belong essentially together. Hence, we can never either conceive or understand anything about him, nor are we able to appreciate properly our own situation, other than only in relation to everything else. So now, after our previous reflections, we nevertheless have to inquire about how matters really

---

5. Eds.—John 14:6a.
6. Eds.—John 14:6b.
7. Eds.—See John 12:32.

stand with ourselves in connection with that childlike confidence in which the Lord commended his soul into the hands of his heavenly Father. Moreover, we immediately have to admit that although steadfastly devoted to him in heartfelt love, although blessed by means of all the benefits of his reconciling death, and indeed as blessed by the whole Christ in such a way that in this respect we should indeed also be like him, nevertheless, when our own time comes, we would then certainly lag behind in the matter of our wills being one with God's will. Hence, we would certainly do well to ask what it was in his own case that immediately preceded this word, and by what means his soul was so in tune with such a pure and heavenly tone.

When we recall here what we specifically reflected on earlier; when we repeat the beautiful words, namely, "Father, forgive them for they do not know what they are doing"; when we remember those matters concerning how he commended his mother to his disciple, and his friend to his mother; when we consider how when thinking about the entire previous life he had led and that was now coming to an end, with its whole series of earlier divine revelations and his cry, "It is finished"; then we certainly realize immediately that this word also necessarily belongs together with that one, and that with regard to us, too, the same tone must lead us if in the same way as our Redeemer we are to be able to say, "Father, into your hands I commend my spirit." How indeed would it even be possible that a person should have attained to this oneness of one's will with God's will if in one's heart one has not made peace with the world which God has created and ordered to be as it is! How is the one who has never come to concord with the will of God in this life able to die in accord with God? Therefore, my good friends, every perversity in this world which anyone who reveres the Lord surely has reason to lament—no matter how severely these may also have affected us, such as through harmful influences in the contexts in which we live our lives—all of these should only seem to us like the illusion that is ever more disappearing from the human soul due to the continuing development of divine grace. That illusion is like the residual insensibility that unfortunately is still to be found in many of our brothers and sisters, yet the heavenly light from above will soon disperse it. And so, we too are to have said, "Father forgive them for they know not what they do," no matter what meets us in life; no matter how little we are able to be supported even in our benevolent concerns and endeavors; no matter how hostile the world may treat us in our eager striving to build the Reign of God!

Just as the Redeemer even still on the cross commended both disciple and mother to each other, at the end of our lives we also have to be engaged in the fitting activity of establishing a genuine and firm bond of a more heartfelt love if not for the first time then indeed to strengthen that bond anew and unite it more earnestly among those who are our neighbors. If these are the wishes that fulfill us, then this is the most valued word toward which even in the final moment of our lives we should also employ our voices and reach out our hands. Then we likewise shall not be lacking in the consciousness of the genuine oneness of will with our heavenly Father in the power of which we in the same way can commend ourselves to God as did the Redeemer. For indeed, what is the being of God other than love? And what more glorious power than this exists to bring about something great and beautiful in the world or when through love we also promote and strengthen love. However, if at life's end it is still our calling to scatter this divine seed in human souls, then we can still rejoice in our exercising some particular influence even if it is no more important and more significant than that which the Redeemer exercised in this moment. This is so, inasmuch as although both were already in Christ and loved one another for his sake, he simply brought the mother and the disciple closer together, and for the sake of their personal and public lives instructed them more explicitly and more specifically.

Hence, we have an immediate consciousness of the powerful indwelling of eternal love in us, and therefore the consciousness of oneness of will with God, which includes yet more than that peace with the order in his world that we have attained by means of a general forgiveness. Now, that is really something far higher and more glorious when we are aware of a positive participation in that whereby everything in the world exists and is advanced, with what should grow and remain permanent inasmuch as we plant the power of love in those whom we leave behind so that they become ever more alert and vigorous in pursuit of the attainment of the goal for which we ourselves can no longer work. And as the Redeemer, all the more confident and at all times more grateful, looked back with these words "It is finished," on the entire course of his life that was now coming to an end and was able to commend himself to his heavenly Father, in the same way it will also be salutary and profitable when in keeping with his understanding we look back at the past thankfully rejoicing in the gentle divine grace that has often led us on to hidden and inscrutable paths but to no other goal than to the excellent goal of salvation. This is so, for when things that were prepared for us and came to be, even those that in this life often could not be explained, we will understand them better at life's end, at which point one thing throws light on the other. Then, with such a view to the past, as our life is coming to a close, we also will become so firm in the confidence that no one can tear us from the hand of the One who has thought so well of us, that we will be able to say just as confidently as the Redeemer, "Father, into your hands I commend my spirit."

Still, my good friends, in no respect would I want to have said this as if to suggest that we should perhaps want to have this experience and practice it as that which secures and alleviates our departure at life's final moment alone. On the contrary, it is precisely by this means that in the most fruitful way our entire life becomes a learning to die when it is filled with this understanding. Every moment of calm reflection that the Lord grants us is therefore an immersion in the divine ways with us and with the whole human race to which we belong. Therefore our life is a continual consent to the great and glorious word of the Lord, "It is finished." It is a life filled with the feeling that now, on our behalf and on behalf of our whole human race, everything is accomplished through Jesus, through his life, his death, and his exaltation. In every moment the life of every pious and faithful disciple of Jesus is also involved in preaching love and establishing love. Indeed, only a slight feeling of harshness and antipathy passes over otherwise calm and gentle souls like a shadow. If such a feeling actually comes to us, it is toward those among our brothers and sisters who are still far from their goal and so wander in the shadow of death. They oppose our endeavors on behalf of the Reign of God in hostile ways. In every such moment, let us be prepared to revert to the feeling that the Redeemer expressed in his blessed prayer, "Father, forgive them for they do not know what they are doing."

For such, my good friends, was also the entire life of the Redeemer. In every significant moment of it, by means of the little of it that has been revealed to us, there is again everywhere mirrored also for us this glorious word with which he departed it. Hence, also for him the end of life could not have been taken to be different from any transition from one day and from one condition to another. And what has he to say to us? The Lord says, "Whoever believes in me has eternal life,"[8] and for whoever has then passed through death to eternal life, death has not only ceased to be something terrifying, but it has also ceased to be anything at all special or vastly different from any other transition. This is so, for each moment that the

---

8. Eds.—John 3:15.

soul of such a person flees faithfully from earthly and transitory things to the eternal, each moment it is separated from the world to immerse itself in the sea of divine love, then in each moment it commends itself—together with the work in which it is engaged or that part of it which it has just accomplished—to the hands into which alone we can commend all things. In this way the spirit then always settles back into its eternal origin. This is the faith that gives us eternal life. Ah yes, once our soul has become united with him, we find it again in every word of the Redeemer—but indeed we most gloriously find it as we celebrate him today, when we accompany him to the cross on which he finished his work, and from which, as at once the climax of his humiliation and the beginning of his exaltation, he also began to draw all of us to himself. May he ever continue to do this with ever greater power so that the blessings of his obedience to death will become more and more widespread among the human race and be ever further glorified in every individual. We, then, will hold firmly to the "pioneer and perfecter of our faith."[9] The more we experience how he "became for us wisdom from God, and righteousness, and sanctification, and redemption,"[10] and also becomes for us wisdom for living and dying, the more faithfully we will ever and again look upon him who as surrendering and dying for sinners, is still in death as in life the same blessed Redeemer, so that we can drink "grace upon grace from his fullness."[11]

Amen.

9. Eds.—Heb 12:2a.
10. Eds.—1 Cor 1:30.
11. Eds.—John 1:16.

8

The Death of the Redeemer as the End of All Sacrifice

Good Friday, April 16, 1824[1]

My devout friends: no matter how deeply our hearts are moved on a day such at this; no matter how unnerved our hearts are by the awareness of sin; and despite even our being permeated by a gratitude for the compassion from above that has decided our salvation and which did not spare its own Son, we will always be certain of having found in this what is right and true only when here we also test our thoughts and feelings in accordance with the measure of Scripture.

Now, with regard to this matter we discover two treatments of this supremely important subject of today's solemn celebration. The accounts of the gospel writers unfold for us the facts of the life and death of Christ. They develop them for us in their individual circumstances, and when the gospels are placed closely side by side, we see in all the features of this story the clearest light of heavenly love and purity as well as the darkest shadows of sin and perversity. Who would not have readily lingered during this time that was especially appointed to reflect upon the sufferings of Christ! And who again now should not also have one's own experiences of the purifying and uplifting power of these sacred accounts! In this regard, the more we keep the matters of the Spirit in view and do not let these be displaced

---

1. This sermon was preached in Holy Trinity Church, Berlin on Good Friday, April 16, 1824, in the morning. The textual basis for the translation is SW II.2 (1843) 161–75. This sermon is also available in KGA III.2, 156–70.

by external considerations that certainly exert a strong sensory power on us, the purer will have been the blessing that was conveyed to us by such a contemplation of Christ's suffering. Now, in their writings to individual brothers and sisters and to Christian congregations the apostles of the Lord already presuppose this acquaintance with the external facts but take every opportunity to draw the attention of Christians to the profoundly mysterious significance of the death of Christ for our salvation, to its connection with the great purpose and goal of redemption, and with the entire treasure of our hopes and our faith. Hence, the more that consideration of the historical and factual matters is appropriate to the preliminary celebration of this important day, which has certainly occupied all pious members of our congregations in this period not only during our assemblies but also in the calm solitude of their devotions, the more it seems natural to me that in this hallowed hour we should turn to one of these apostolic declarations and devote our reflections to the profound significance of the death of Christ for the salvation of human beings. Therefore, in hymns and in the Lord's Prayer let us pray for God's blessing and support.

Text: Hebrews 10:8–12

> When he said above, 'You have neither desired nor taken pleasure in sacrifices and offerings and burnt-offerings and sin-offerings' (these are offered according to the law), then he added, 'See, I have come to do your will.' He abolishes the first in order to establish the second. And it is by God's will that we have been sanctified through the offering of the body of Jesus Christ once for all. And every priest stands day after day at his service, offering again and again the same sacrifices that can never take away sins. But when Christ had offered for all time a single sacrifice for sins, 'he sat down at the right hand of God'.

My devout friends, from the entire context of these words it follows very clearly that the godly author views the death of the Redeemer as the real turning point at which the old covenant came to an end and from which the new covenant of God with human beings took its beginning. Inasmuch as he presents the death of the Redeemer as a sacrifice for sin, at the same time, in that he says that by means of a single sacrifice all such sacrifices are brought to an end, he also presents it as the end of all sacrifice and of all worship by means of sacrifices. This was the situation when both were practiced in the times before the Redeemer as well as in the worship services of the Jewish people, and as also was the case in the sacred rites of other nations when they were mixed with a great deal of illusion and error, but in all of which such sacrificial practices constituted what was essential. And here the two are placed in sharpest contrast with each other, on the one hand, the inadequacy of all earlier sacrifices, and on the other, that eternal divine power by means of which the sacrifice of the Redeemer surpasses all of them and which precisely for this reason brought an end to all other sacrifices. Hence, so understood, and as present here together, let us consider the matter of the death of Christ as the end of all sacrifice.

In earlier statements of this chapter which precede our text the author had already said that sacrifices would have ceased if those persons present at worship no longer had any consciousness of sin but were cleansed once for all, but in these sacrifices there is a reminder of sin "year after year." (v. 2) But as he states in our text, by means of the repetition of sacrifices sin itself can never be taken away. Therefore, we will deal not only with the meaning of his statements but also make a thorough examination of their substance to the extent that we view the death of the Redeemer as the end of all sacrifice, first because now no memorial of sin that has to be repeated from one day to another and from one year to another is any longer necessary; and then secondly, because now that sin has truly been taken away, such inadequate representative expedients are no longer necessary. Hence, let us now direct our prayerful attention to these two aspects.

I

So, my good friends, at first sacrifices were a memorial of sin; now, however, since Christ became a sacrifice for sin, no other memorial of sin is any longer necessary.

In what way, then, my good friends, were the sacrifices of the old covenant a memorial of sin? They were of such a kind that by means of the sacrifice for individual actions at variance with the laws of the Highest One a satisfaction had to be made so that anxiety about further rebukes and punishments would cease. Moreover, and in fact at the same time, through the presentation of the sacrifice a confession of the action deserving punishment would be made so that for the sins of every individual, for that in which he himself had fallen short with regard to the law, there would be established a memorial by means of the public presentation of the sacrifice. We can stop at this point, my good friends, simply to note what an imperfect action this was. For what in fact are the individual actions of human beings in which sin is revealed in relation to sin itself? They are nothing other than random outbreaks of inward corruption that are dependent on external circumstances in a thousand different ways.

Suppose we place two people side by side, one of whom on one and the same day had a good many of such outward offenses for which to repent and make amends, and the other could boast that he or she had not committed a single act of this kind. On this account is the one better than the other? By no means! Rather, the one had merely hit upon a favorable time; the other, by contrast, on an unpropitious one. But corruption itself dwells just as deeply and just as firmly in the soul of the one as in that of the other. Indeed, this is how we have to view the matter! How in fact is it possible for a person to sort out the individual actions that he or she performs and claim them as his or her own? Of course, in his or her innermost feeling a person can always be right to ascribe to oneself an action he or she has committed that is criminal and punishable without appealing to anyone else. However, it would be wrong for others to absolve themselves on his or her account in such a way and to think that they are cleared of all guilt in relation to the action of the other since it is assigned to the guilty party alone. Hence, he would not at all times be completely wrong to implicate others in his guilt such as those nearer, more distant, and often those, who knows how far distant.

No, my good friends! If we simply seek the truth at all and look into the manifold entanglements of life, and are conscious of all the overt and hidden influences that one person exercises on another, then we will readily confirm that indirectly or directly each person has a part in the sins that manifest themselves in others, and that in no respect can we settle our account only with regard to those sins that we ourselves have committed. Ah yes, manifold indeed, not only through tempting examples and through careless speech, but also through well-intentioned and palliative judgments, through neglected reprimands. In these and in so many other different ways we each assist the other in bringing forth sins, none of which indeed appertains to one person alone. Hence, this is why every memorial of sin with regard to sacrifices was so imperfect and inadequate, because it rested on this division of human accountability, and because it comprehends sin only where it appears externally. The consequence of this is that in this way its inner reality is not at all established in memory in conformity with the truth. Moreover, when elsewhere the apostle states that "the knowledge of sin comes by the law,"[2] he is absolutely right because this in fact is the highest merit that can be attributed to an external law when it is often so certain that there is no power within it to effect any genuine improvement. But with this statement he could in no respect have intended to mean that the memorial of sin which was established in the law as the required sacrifice could ever have brought forth a perfect consciousness or a genuine knowledge of sin. No, first and foremost this genuine knowledge of sin is also wholly derived from the perspective of the suffering and dying Redeemer. Hence, it is from one and the same perspective that we are shown the full depth of the human corruption that initiated this death, as well as the entire glory of the only begotten Son of the Father, so that with complete justification we can say that there is no other true memorial of sin than that of the death of the Lord. Here it accomplished its greatest work; here it is shown in its full power and perfection.

The apostle John also certainly considered this matter when he summed up all sin under the expressions "the desire of the eyes," "the desire of the flesh," and "the haughty life."[3] The desire of the eyes, namely, the perverse inclination of human beings to let themselves be ensnared by outward appearance and to judge the inner life accordingly. This was the reason why so many among the Lord's contemporaries let themselves be led astray by such superficial judgments such as "What good can come out of Nazareth?"[4] What does this person want to imply himself to be who has not studied Scripture like the rest of us? "The desire of the flesh," namely, the satisfaction of human beings in the transitory pleasures of temporal life, the striving after esteem and honor in the world, holding firmly to and increasing external possessions, and the joy in seeing that others are dependent on one and, accordingly, one's being honored by them. This was the reason why the high priests and elders of his people decided among themselves that "it is better for you to have one man die than to have the whole nation destroyed,"[5] Based on the arrogant self-confidence of human beings. "the haughty life" is certainly that

---

2. Eds.—Rom 3:20.

3. 1 John 2:16. Eds.—This is our translation of Schleiermacher who is directly quoting short phrases from the biblical text cited.

4. Eds.—John 1:46.

5. Eds.—John 11:50. Schleiermacher adds "for thereby we can bridle and direct the people."

of one who supposes that in insight and way of life such a one has already laid hold of what is best and most perfect, and so regards everything based on this supposition to be so unsurpassable as to prevent the entry of anything better. Hence, in this pleasant twilight of complacency every pure light is scorned and spurned. And this was the reason why the wise and powerful of that time certainly did not believe John's intimations of the Reign of God, and also thereafter why the mystery of the divine decrees remained hidden from them and could be revealed only to the childlike. But it was precisely for this reason that it remained hidden to the wise and powerful among the people, and that thereby they could sin in such a way against the content of all the promises so that they crucified Christ. Hence, we can now rightly say that, with respect to everything darkening the human soul and alienating human beings from the way of salvation and truth, we find the clearest mirror of the circumstances of guilt involved in the death of the Redeemer. This is so, in that thereby an indelible memorial of sin was established for all eternity, so that among the only nation in which the knowledge of the one God was preserved, precisely those persons who should have been its most preeminent possessors and upholders were sinful and corrupt enough to nail the Prince of life and the Lord of glory to the cross. What further need do we have of a memorial for sin? There it was raised "once for all,"[6] in such a way as for all time and for the whole human race, and also equally so for every single individual heart and mind.

This is so, for that which still moves us to sin, that which is still in us that strives against obedience to the will of God of which Christ was the eternal image, can always be referred back to something that has to do with having been made guilty of the death of the Lord so that we will have to view all sin as contributing to his crucifixion. Therefore, just as little as we, will every future generation also require a different memorial of sin from this one which was established in the death of the Lord. For this reason it is the end of all sacrifices, because the melancholy confession of individual sins by means of such sacred practices, and of course above all the sorrow and regret for particular outbreaks of corruption, of whatever kind they may be, can certainly in no respect be compared with Jesus' suffering. All of us, without distinction between better and worse, have to bow down before his suffering since it was our sins—those of people like us and we like them—and the common corruption that we also find in ourselves that crucified the Lord of glory. A memorial that in such a

---

6. Eds.—Heb 10:10b.

way embraces everything in the human soul that is perverse renders every other memorial forever superfluous.

Nevertheless, again with regard to individual sinful actions we have committed—that we have imposed on ourselves or allowed to be imposed on us, actions such as works of love or devotional disciplines, which also certainly cannot undo what once has been done—we can in no way block the sinful sources of such actions, and these can therefore also be nothing other than a memorial of sin. What else can we do but revert to that imperfect condition which possessed only the shadow instead of the essence? And by this means what can we also prove other than that we do not place the proper value on the memorial of sin which was secured for us in the sacrifice of Christ? Hence, may today's solemn celebration of the death of Christ firmly establish us anew on this foundation of the faith of our church so that in this connection we also look back to nothing other than the perfect sacrifice of Christ that happened once for all on the cross. Therefore, all who admonish their hearts to consider the corruption in their own breasts, and everyone to whom the sin established of old still returns with its particular signs, let them cast themselves down before the cross of Christ and there entreat the Father in the name of the One who was made the sacrifice for sin to preserve them from sin and not also to crucify again the Lord of glory and the Prince of life with the desire of their eyes, the desire of their flesh, or their arrogant life.

II

Now, each sacrifice of the Old Covenant, as often as it is repeated, was ever and only an imperfect memorial of sin. Second, on this account the sacrifices were much less able to take away sins. But inasmuch as together with confession they were able only to renew and preserve the memorial of sin, the life of sin and its power always remained the same. Hence, they merely supported the longing for another help, and also the wish that such a help would finally appear, and should it also come down from heaven, that it would in fact even be able to take away sin itself and its power. Therefore, in that the author of our letter says that the death of the Redeemer is the end of all sacrifices, this above all is now his understanding, namely, that through the death of the Lord and to the extent that it was a sacrifice, sin itself is also taken away so that no further sacrifice is necessary. As he states in the words that follow:

"Let us then approach with a true heart in full assurance of faith, with our hearts sprinkled clean from an evil conscience."[7]

But in what way and in what sense is sin taken away through the death of the Redeemer? This, my good friends, as Scripture expresses it, is the great mystery of existing in fellowship with him in his death and in his life. These two facts, then, that we are buried with him in his death and that we also rise with him to a new life,[8] both of these aspects, my good friends, cannot be separated from true faith in the Redeemer. This is so, for what does it mean to believe in him if it does not at least mean to acknowledge him as the promised Savior of human beings, as the One who could show the right way to those who had gone astray, and who could bring life to those who had died because he himself was the truth and because in him sin had no place? But if we acknowledge him in this way, how should we, on account of his death, not also die to everything that brought about his death? Accordingly, we can certainly want nothing other than his life, but only the human nature to the extent that it is receptive to the influence of his spiritual power so that this will be spread abroad upon the whole human race. Those who believed could have had no wish to kill the Redeemer; therefore, it has to be with faith—if not it is no faith—that people renounce everything that brought about the Redeemer's death. And in this way the old self reckons as crucified with Christ everything in us that makes manifest the power of sin.

But not only this, for just as essentially it belongs to faith in him that we accept his life into ourselves so that with the apostle we can say: "It is no longer I who live, but it is Christ who lives in me."[9] Because, my good friends, this belongs to the essence of persons: to seek to remain in communion with the One through whose breath Christ has become a rational soul. In times of the most profound corruption and of the thickest darkness, persons have not been entirely capable of renouncing this longing to be conscious of the Highest Being and to unite their existence to him. But rather, on account of the fact that they had once lost the true path, they have preferred—as the apostle says—to devote their veneration to transient images of the creation, and thus they worshiped the creation

---

7. Eds.—Heb 10:22.
8. Eds.—See Rom 6:4.
9. Gal 2:20.

instead of the Creator, as if they had to completely surrender that most essential and highest need.[10]

Hence, when even in the frivolous fables about false gods and also in the gloomy illusions of idol worship and indeed in all the misanthropic horrors that have developed from these, we nevertheless cannot fail to recognize the striving of human beings after the divine being. Moreover, we also certainly have to grant that for an enlightened heart and mind there cannot be a deeper pain than that of seeing that which is most sacred being deformed and misused in such a way. Was it indeed not altogether natural that this striving had to develop and be guided into the right way when the Father revealed himself in the Son, when the divine Word became flesh, and when the teacher who shows the Father appeared in human form, when the divine love became visible in the glory of the only begotten Son who is its image? And is it not indeed the case that the Son knew nothing else and lived in nothing other than this striving to share all that he had received with his brothers and sisters, and to draw everyone to himself and into his life as being fully one with the Father? This is so, for in the human soul there was nothing more than need and longing that could be of help to the Redeemer. Real insight into the truth, the desire for the good—neither existed. Yet, inasmuch as both belonged to the soul, in directly addressing them and arousing them, the power of his divine actions also needed no more than these.

Therefore, what happened was that those who knew him in faith not only died with him to the old self but also rose with him to a new life, namely, to his singular life which he readily shared, and then they were ever anew strengthened and nourished by means of every word of wisdom from his lips and every glance of divine gentleness and love from his eyes. These quickening activities are again now firmly established in the Christian church through the preached Word of Scripture and through the divine Spirit which demonstrates its effectiveness by means of these. On the other hand, viewed in and of themselves, the works of creation, although our knowledge of them has significantly increased as experience sufficiently teaches, have not at all become more powerful in making God more known to us and in leading us to him as was formerly the case. Nevertheless, it still happens that the Father reveals himself to us only in the Son, and the mystery of the communication of this continues in the same way inasmuch as with the Redeemer we also

---

10. Eds.—See Rom 1:25.

rise to new life, but only after we have been buried with him in his death and therefore always in conjunction with this.

Hence, my good friends, in that in this sense we are crucified with Christ and have risen with him to a new life, sin is in truth taken away. For not only is the consciousness of it—or as the author of our text expresses it, "the conscience of sin,"—destroyed, but also its guilt is canceled.

Now, concerning the first we can certainly say that the person who has died to sin and to the law, since both had a role in the Lord's crucifixion, has also precisely for this reason lost the consciousness of sin to the extent that his or her will has renounced its power as well as having any part in it. And, the person who has risen with the Redeemer to a new life, in that person Christ alone lives and is formed in him ever more completely. This one, whose self—that is whose previous self—no longer lives, this person has lost the consciousness of sin insofar as such a person has received another consciousness, precisely that of this life in community with Christ, who would want nothing other than to do the will of his heavenly Father. And just as in this connection no sin whatever existed in Christ himself, with the consciousness that he lives in us there also exists no consciousness of sin. Much rather is it the case that just as Christ's life was one of blessedness so also is our consciousness nothing other than blessedness to the extent that we are united with him. This is so, for whenever the innermost will is in accord with the undivided will of God, as far as we are perhaps able to recognize it at all and have a sense of it, then here there can be nothing that disturbs or upsets. Since even what is still remaining in us as a result of weakness—because it finally finds no support in our wills—really no longer belongs to our actual life at all but to that remaining outside of us on account of which we are to fight the good fight of faith. In this way we truly feel blessed in that we act as the instruments of God and in his power. Therefore, it is true that we are free from the conscience of sin precisely according to the measure in which Christ lives in us. Hence, my good friends, this is certainly something about which, on the one hand, we indeed can and must say, "Not that I have already attained this or reached this goal, but I press onto make it my own,"[11] on the other hand we nevertheless surely have to admit and praise God for the fact that it is the deepest, clearest, and most pure truth that even now already exists in life and in the hearts of Christians. To be united with Christ is nothing other

---

11. Eds.—Phil 3:12.

than blessedness in us, pure joy in the Lord, the inward communion with his and with our Father in heaven.

However, someone could say, all of this granted, how does it happen? How, exactly, is it that this renewed consciousness drives out the conscience of sin in us through the death of the Redeemer? Now, evidently his disciples indeed had faith in him as the Son of the living God as well as having the inward joy in the words of life that were exclusively at his disposal. Consequently, they also had that relationship with him in the course of their life together already prior to his death! Yet, from the outset of his public life and activity there certainly existed the presentiment and consciousness of his death, in fact precisely this death, so that we have to say that he always acted in the power of his death. It was after his resurrection that Christ was first able to make his disciples understand that he had to suffer this death in order to enter his glory. This was always equally deeply impressed upon him, and it was out of this conviction that he spoke and acted through his entire public life. Moreover, in this way the power of his death was already present for a long time in his disciples before they were clearly made aware of it. Indeed it was only as they saw him who alone had no part in sin in this strong opposition to the sin of the world—only because he would be revealed to them as the Lamb of God who bore the sins of the world,[12] from the beginning—that this true and living belief in him as the Redeemer could rise in the souls of his disciples. Therefore, as far as we also are concerned, still even much less is the power of his death to be separated from the power of his life.

Yet in that we are crucified with the Lord and have risen with him to new life, it is not only the consciousness of sin that is taken away, but the guilt of sin is also canceled as also is God's judgment upon us so that the relationship to the Highest Being, with regard to which sin is the obstacle to us, has become different. This is also what the author of our letter means when as Scripture states, he says, "Sacrifices and burnt offerings you have not desired. They do not please you." And he adds, "in the scroll of the book it is written of me, 'I have come to do your will, O God'"[13]—and here the Lord who says this, and who let it be said, abolishes the one and upholds the other. This is so, because that which has been abolished is in fact the ordinance of the sacrifice which cannot blot out the guilt of sin. Now, this guilt consists in the fact that setting one's mind on the

---

12. Eds.—John 1:29.
13. Eds.—See Heb 10:5–7.

things of the flesh[14] is enmity against God. However, the person who has died to sin and to the law with Christ and who has risen to a new life still of course continues to live in the flesh, and this he cannot and will not be able to deny throughout the course of his entire earthly life. Nevertheless, he no longer lives according to the flesh, his hostility to God has been abolished, and those to whom the Son has given the power to become God's children because they believe in him, now also love God in the most beloved Son. Moreover, when in what follows the author says, "This is the covenant I will make with them after those days . . . I will put my laws in their hearts, and I will write them on their minds" (Heb 10:16), this is nothing other than what has just been described as the natural and simple consequence of our life in community with the Redeemer. And we want to ask everyone to pay attention to these words so that no one will interpret our view to mean that the guilt of sin can be taken away by a mere wish for improvement, however sincere that wish may be. This is so, for a wish, even without reserve, is still something completely empty and futile and leaves everything in the human being in that which was formerly the case and in that which is past, so that God's judgment has to remain the judgment that is past and the guilt remain the guilt that is past. If I may say so, it is always only with the lips of the soul that the person who has a wish turns to God, and not with the innermost heart. But the fact that God's will is written in the heart as well as in the mind, this indeed means so much more. Such is the case, for then the struggle and strivings of human beings are those that arise from the most inward active disposition and are directed towards the will of God, and what the minds of human beings most favor in the world is simply to give attention to what it is that relates to them. Therefore, whatever vestige of weakness that still remains in human beings as the consequence of past sin is in them only against their will. Nevertheless, as completely one with God's will, his will is directed against all sin; and when in this way the will as a whole is directed against sin as a whole, then guilt is also taken away. This is so, for that which really happens contrary to the will is not ascribed to anyone's account. This will is simply the communion with the One who came to destroy the reign of sin. But we also arrive at this will only in that we are joined to Christ so that his will which alone is pure is communicated to us. Love of Christ and the good fight of the will as a whole against sin are one and the same. But every attempt by ourselves or others

---

14. Eds.—See Rom 8:1–8.

to better ourselves by ourselves and apart from communion with the Redeemer not only is fragmentary but also falls so far short of the very least of what we should do—which is not to be distinguished from the empty wish that cannot discern the judgment of God.

Therefore, when we build the Reign of God and work against all the sin that is both within us and external to us with the powers we have—that admittedly to this point have certainly been entirely limited, although they will become abundant and strong through the One who alone is able to strengthen us—then the guilt of sin is taken away. Consequently, God no longer sees us as each of us was in one's self and will so remain, but rather sees us only in the Beloved and as the persons we have become through him. Indeed, in accordance with this new covenant the will of God is given to our hearts and written in our minds so that God is also no longer able to be mindful of our unrighteousness and our sin but regards only the new life that we live in his Son as our own.

My good friends, according to the words of our text let us now sum up the author's real meaning: the death of Christ is a sacrifice which he offered for sin because voluntary obedience to death on the cross is the highest point of all obedience. The obedience of the Redeemer and the sacrifice he offered are not two different things but are one and the same. But everything is imperfect in our understanding and in our description of our relationship to God, every external condition, every other sacrifice and practice of purification finds its final closure in the hallowed death of the Redeemer. Inasmuch as in his death we see in him above all the glory of the only begotten Son of the Father, and yet also the power to which sin had elevated itself to the level of enmity against God, then for all of us it is precisely on account of the fact that with Christ we have died with him to that which is imperfect; old things have passed away, and a new life together has begun that in communion with the Redeemer aspires to true holiness and righteousness.[15] Yet, the more we wish that this life will be ever more effective and be spread more widely abroad, the more thankfully we will again and again return to the death of the Lord as the eternal memorial of sin which ever anew demands that all of us die to sin, and to the death of the Lord as the sole sacrifice through which all are blessed who here are sanctified. Indeed, my good friends, you are those who are sanctified, all those who remain, and grow and flourish in the life that the Redeemer has kindled within them. You are those who in deed and truth

---

15. Eds.—See 2 Cor 5:17.

ever more renounce all participation in sin and all trust in the law and in the works of the law ever more build themselves up to be one spiritual body of Christ among themselves. You are those who are sanctified here once and for all, made perfect by means of the sacrifice which he has offered, and even though their obedience appears to be less perfect, it is nevertheless an outpouring from the perfect obedience of Christ and is one with this obedience. You are those who are forever made perfect precisely so that now you can be sanctified in a new life now that the conscience of sin and the guilt of sin have been taken away from you, and you have become participants in the freedom of the children of God, the only place in which the true good can prosper. Therefore, as the apostle Paul says, it is now simply the case that "There is therefore, now no condemnation for those who are in Christ Jesus,"[16] and we can give thanks to God, who has rescued us from this body of death,[17] and given us the victory through our Lord Jesus Christ.[18] We owe it to his sacrifice which he offered once for all for sin, that the guilt and consciousness of sin has been taken away from us so that now we no longer may live as participants in the sin that crucified him, but rather in glorious and blessed communion with Christ himself.

Therefore, my good friends, with regard to the memorial of the death of Jesus what could we offer other than hearts that are deeply moved and thankful! When we consider the sacrifice that is eternally valid, how could we do otherwise than present ourselves ever more as a sacrifice that here will be one that is living, holy, and pleasing to God![19] How could we do otherwise—owing to this eternal and indelible recollection of sin—than continually ground ourselves ever more firmly in holy enmity against all that is in enmity with God and the will of God?" How indeed otherwise than by clothing ourselves ever more in the righteousness and love of the One who gave up his life for us all even when we were still sinners and enemies,[20] and also by embracing with the same love those who are still constrained by hostility against God and so attract them and draw them into the salvation of reconciliation! How could we do otherwise than call to him all those who still toil in false and unfruitful duties as those who "labor

---

16. Eds.—Rom 8:1.

17. Eds.—Rom 7:24–25.

18. Rom 8:1, 7:24, 25. Eds.—See also 1 Cor 5:57.

19. Rom 12:1. Eds.—This is our translation of Schleiermacher who is not directly quoting the biblical text.

20. Eds.—See Rom 5:8.

and are heavy laden,"[21] to him in whom they will find quickening and peace for their souls when in the proper sense they let themselves be directed toward the one and eternally valid sacrifice through which everyone can be made perfect! And so, let us praise in word and deed the one who through life and death has become for us very much both salvation and sanctification as well as wisdom and righteousness. Amen.

Prayer: Indeed, merciful God and Father, you who have not turned aside from the sinful world but in accordance with your eternal love have concluded everything under sin so that you may have mercy on all; praise and thanksgiving be unto you that in your Son you have been mindful of us, and that through him you have reconciled us to yourself to open for us the way to the blessed communion we have with you and in which we rejoice in him. Oh rule more widely over the Reign of your Son on earth so that he may obtain still more as the reward of his life and death and that of these many more will always increase who will find life and blessedness in him. And establish all those who already have come to the healing salutary knowledge of Christ ever more firmly in the hallowed bond of faith and love so that the word may prove ever more true that we have died with him to sin and to the external law, and that the life from God, which he alone can bring, is ever more gloriously revealed in us all. For letting us enjoy these fruits of his death we stand beside you in childlike humility. Your desire is to let them flourish more and more abundantly on earth so that the glory of the Crucified One will become ever more glorious until everyone will kneel before him to receive from him what your fatherly love and mercy have accomplished through him. Amen.

---

21. Eds.—Matt 11:28.

9

A Consideration of the Circumstances that Accompanied the Final Moments of the Redeemer

Good Friday, April 20, 1821[1]

Praise and thanks to him who raised the Redeemer on the cross to be a saving sign and also to glorify him with such heavenly brightness! Praise and honor to him who by his obedience to death became the pioneer of faith so that as a true high priest he could represent before God those whom he was not ashamed to call his brothers and sisters. Amen.

Text: Luke 23:44–49

It was now about noon, and darkness came over the whole land until three in the afternoon, while the sun's light failed; and the curtain of the temple was torn in two. Then Jesus, crying with a loud voice, said, "Father into your hands I commend my spirit." Having said this he breathed his last. When the centurion saw what had taken place, he praised God and said, "Certainly this man was innocent." And when all the crowds who had gathered there for this spectacle saw what had taken place, they returned home, beating their breasts. But all his acquaintances, including the women who had followed him from Galilee, stood at a distance, watching these things.

---

1. This sermon was preached in the Cathedral Church, Berlin on Good Friday, April 20, 1821, in the morning. The textual basis for the translation is SW II.2 (1843) 442–51. This sermon is also available in KGA III.2, 594–603.

JESUS' LIFE IN DYING

My devout friends, the propensity to find great events to be accompanied by extraordinary signs as well is long established and universal. Indeed, even if a dearth of signs should not disturb our faith, we nevertheless lack a certain satisfaction, and we would take it to be odd if everything that contributed to the important subject of today's celebration was not equally rich in significance for the entire course and development of the work of Christ and for the great purpose that God the heavenly Father sought to accomplish through his death. But what we find is exactly this richness! When we consider the sad and painful drama of Christ's death, we see him surrounded there by brutal enemies until his final moment. Nevertheless, counteracting this, to the alert eye there radiates the great and the sublime, and to its comfort and quickening the faithful heart received signs from above. With this in mind, let us then together in this sacred hour also consider the conditions that accompanied the Redeemer's final moments. In this way we are strengthened anew by his death and by the hope that arises from it, and so our confident vision of its blessed consequences will expand still further. However, as far as our reflections are concerned, we will first isolate the external signs accompanying the death of the Redeemer, then we will examine what our Gospel account reports in connection with the effects of these on people's hearts and minds. These are the two parts of our reflection to which I would like you to give your Christian attention.

I

My good friends, when we consider the signs that accompanied the death of our Redeemer we are overcome with the sense of a great and mysterious interconnection between the realm of nature and the realm of the Spirit and of grace. With regard to every such interrelationship between these two realms our attention is directed to everything of importance that occurs in the human world. To inquire into this is certainly a dangerous tendency for those who are still little acquainted with the things of nature. They succumb to an anxious tension with regard to all the unusual events of nature as to what they may in fact signify for the spiritual world. Yet regardless of the propriety of warning against this, it is entirely different when viewed from the opposite direction and for those who alert to everything that belongs to the spiritual world. Then it is a matter of the stirring of the most delicate feeling when we are on the lookout for accompanying signs in nature that correspond to the importance of the spiritual event. To discover this interconnection in the great course of the world's governance is the ultimate and highest goal of the most profound human knowledge and wisdom. But also in particular things, when something important happens in the domain of the spirit, whether indeed it is good or pernicious, it is only the most sensitive conscience that teaches us to search for significant signs in nature. Was it not precisely this consciousness of the divine in Christ that, as it were, compelled so many to recognize a sign of his more exalted honor and destiny in the marvelous deeds that he accomplished? Here, this interconnection is now again made evident to us at his death as of great importance, first in the complete darkness that caused the sun's light to fail, and then in the rending of the curtain in the temple.

"It was about noon," the evangelist writes, "and darkness came over the whole land until three in the afternoon, while the sun's light failed." This darkness was not of the kind that regularly follows the course of our world preceded by its accompanying stars. It was an extraordinary manifestation of nature, and the whole land was covered in darkness. The sun lost its light until three in the afternoon when the Redeemer expired. It was then, and this is really the most significant point, that this darkness ceased and the sun that had been blotted out shone again in its brightness and spread abroad its beneficent light anew.

Oh my dear friends, that which made the Redeemer's appearance on earth absolutely necessary was the sad and universal darkness of the human spirit on account of error, illusion, and sin. But this was still a special instance, one not to be easily explained on the basis of the laws of human nature as occurring everywhere, but rather an extraordinary darkening of human spirits which on the pretext of the divine law nevertheless put to death the man who was mighty in words and deeds, who taught here with spirit and power, and went about to set free those whose spirits had been made captive and miraculously healed the sick. Moreover, even now our experience of nature underscores that such a darkness is a most unusual loss of the sun's luminosity. But that its light broke forth again in the death of the Redeemer—this indeed is now a sign to us, one more glorious than the rainbow of peace that Noah beheld in the clouds after the waters of the flood had receded! As the Lord said there: "this is the sign of the covenant that I make between me and you . . . and waters shall never again become a flood to destroy all flesh on earth."[2] Here, the eternal One also speaks to us inasmuch as that after the death of the Redeemer the light of the darkened sun broke

2. Eds.—Gen 9:12a, 15b.

forth again: let this be a sign between me and you that the darkening of the human soul is now dispersed and done with. The light came from heaven and shone in the darkness. Even though the darkness did not yet receive it, and a great many of the most darkened hearts and minds stood gathered around the cross of the Redeemer, the heavenly light was now made innate in human nature. His Reign was established, and through the gracious decree of God it was ascertained that this heavenly light that proceeded at that time from such an unlikely point should ever more spread abroad among the human race, and that warmed and ignited by the power of this light faith should overcome the world with all its darkness.

Moreover, my dearly beloved, in the history of the gospel's development and of the Reign of God times of darkness have certainly often recurred. Indeed, those who confessed the light that appeared in Christ Jesus were often put to death by the children of darkness just like him. But the servant cannot fare better than the Lord.[3] We have to give less attention to this darkening that set about its work on those who were in fact chosen even though of course they were nevertheless weak and sinful instruments of the Highest and give more attention to the anointed of the Lord, on whom darkness works. For that reason, it remains the case that the fact that this darkness ceased was the great turning point in human history and in the development of their spirits. From Adam onward the Spirit held sway, increasing and advancing according to the innate revelation of God in the hearts of human beings. Nevertheless, it was unable to banish the darkness completely. This is so, for from the very beginning the flesh lusted against the spirit and was pleased to exist in darkness and suppress the truth in unrighteousness.[4] In this ever-recurring struggle, divine voices were always at hand to be of help, but the victory of light over darkness was first decided in the death of the Lord: the Reign of light was established and thereby the work of the Lord accomplished. Hence, those who are buried with him in his death also rise with him to new life. Those who renounce the darkness of sin that nailed the Prince of life to the cross are those in whom his life is glorified in ever increasing brightness.

"And the curtain of the temple was torn in two." This curtain, my good friends, hid the mysteries of the old covenant from the eyes of all people, with the exception of one person who nevertheless could enter only once a year into the Holy of Holies to sprinkle the blood of the covenant there.

3. Eds.—Matt 10:24a.
4. Eds.—Rom 1:18.

Just as the outer curtain separated the priests of the Lord from the people as a whole, in the same way this inner one separated the chief of the priesthood from the rest of his colleagues. Now, inasmuch as this curtain was torn in two it was thereby indicated that, on the one hand, all the mysteries of God were now revealed, and everything hidden had to be uncovered. It was indicated that the particular divine decree and interpretations of the divine will emerging from a place of darkness would no longer be made known to people in a secretive way but that a single decree of salvation should be openly preached to everyone. On the other hand, it was thereby demonstrated that distinctions and gradations should no longer continue among those who worshiped in and through his Son, but that the time had now come when every person in Christ had free access to God, when all believers were priests of the most High, and all were taught by God, and as servants in the Lord each reciprocally served the other. These two matters, my devout friends, namely, that every special priesthood had come to an end, and that now the whole will of God is made known, cannot be separated from one another. Moreover, only in the relationship of both do we have complete confidence of reconciliation effected by the power of the gospel. Before he fell into the hands of his enemies, Christ could offer the proof that he himself gave and that he imparted to his own all the words that he had received from his Father. How could certainty about this, namely, that as the well-beloved Son of God's he had also received the entire fullness of God's self-communication that guarantees to the human soul a blessed communion with God; how could this be more clearly expressed other than that on account of this that curtain was torn in two, demonstrating that now there is no longer any hidden dwelling place of God among human beings. There is no longer a hidden place like that which had prevailed until this point, during which time faith sought the presence of the Most High exclusively above the cover of the ark of the covenant, under which everything was hidden! On the contrary, since Christ entered the true Holy of Holies after the completion of his work in shedding his blood on the cross, his Reign is now the boundless, spiritual house of God in which he himself is appointed as the throne of grace, as the place of the full presence of God among human beings. Although his disciples also felt it sounded somewhat strange that during his lifetime, they should see the Father in the Son,[5] his having completed his work by his obedience to death and his having been exalted, we now recognize in him the true image of

---

5. Eds.—John 14:9b.

the divine being and the reflected splendor of eternal love. Hence, to what purpose should there still be any human mediation or representation? Here there is nothing to behold other than the One to whom honor is due, and to this throne of grace everyone has access! And it is in this way that Christ has become our brother in that he descended to us and took on flesh and blood, and hence we are now his siblings inasmuch as he draws us up to himself, into the same spiritual nearness of the Father. Therefore, the fact is that we are all members of God's household and as such equal with one another. Through him all of us are children of the One who has reconciled us, and all of us members of his spiritual body through his Spirit which he sends into the hearts of believers. Therefore, my good friends, every curtain is torn, and it is the Redeemer on the cross to whom everyone can raise the same confident eyes of faith; it is the exalted Lord from whom all of us directly receive the blessing in spiritual benefits, which the priests of the old covenant certainly wished for but were unable to provide.

These, my dear friends, are the comforting signs that our faith perceives in the death of the Lord. But these signs of peace and grace can reach their fulfillment only through the power of the gospel to bless the hearts of human beings. In this way the gospel was spread abroad from that eternally significant moment in which we rejoice and find comfort when we examine the history of the Christian church up to the present day. Yet, as far as our pious wishes are concerned, the expansion of this blessed Reign still advances only too slowly. We still see too much darkness on this earth into which the light has not penetrated. Yet also with regard to this slow progress we also see reassuring and clear signs when we give heed to what occurred in the hearts and minds of human beings in connection with the death of the Redeemer. But let us now continue and direct our attention to this matter.

II

"When the centurion saw what had taken place, he praised God and said, 'Certainly this man was innocent.'" What then was it, my good friends, that happened before his eyes that could have given rise to this cry? He saw that the darkness had descended and that the sun lost its light. He saw how surprisingly quickly it ended when it seemed to be the case that prolonged torments would still be in store for him. He saw and heard how Jesus, who was accused of such crimes that most upset all calm and peace among human beings, commended his spirit into the hands of the heavenly Father with his soul in complete peace—then the centurion said, "Certainly this man was innocent!" And yet, this rough warrior previously concerned himself little with the commotions that the appearance of the Lord had caused among the people of the Jews, who were wholly alien to him, and whom he despised.

Here, then, we should see this effect on the centurion, even should it have been simply a passing one, a transition from the most extreme indifference toward the death of the Redeemer to its acknowledgement by an excited heart and mind. Another evangelist reports the man's words in this way: "Truly, this man was God's Son!"[6] just as the high priests had also accused him in front of the Roman governor of having himself claimed this status.[7] But now that this had certainly been made known to the centurion, and both of these matters considered, we can indeed conclude that having maintained his post from the point at which Christ was led out, there was tension in his soul between the opinion of Christ's accusers and that impression made by the person of the Redeemer. Nevertheless, when this latter understanding gained the upper hand, in addition to the question of whether he was a pious man delivered over to death by his enemies as an innocent man, it was also asked if he, having now departed this earthly life among such significant signs and in such a glorious way, was in truth the Son of God.

Oh blessed doubt that arises in a soul which hitherto has remained in darkness! Oh the sudden awakening of the spirit from the deepest darkness to absorb the heavenly light which lies in the faith that the Word became flesh and that the Son of the Highest has appeared in human form. Precisely in this way, my good friends—thanks be to God—the proclamation of our Lord's death still continues to make its effect in its own peculiar way. If souls in complete darkness are to be initiated into the mysteries of the Reign of God—that is, if to those who still wander in the shadow of death the Reign of heaven is closed, then nothing else matters than proclaiming the dying Redeemer to human beings. From time immemorial the image of his death has been the most powerful Word of life. Where a heart and mind by faith sketch this picture, there indeed indifferent souls are often awakened. And if only they say first of all, "Certainly this was an innocent man," and afterwards hear his own words about the glory he had always had with the Father, and they next hear the stories

6. Eds.—Mark 15:39b.
7. Eds.—Mark 15:1–2.

about his life and the efficacy of his resurrection, then they will also soon say with all of us, "Truly, this is God's Son!"

"And when all the crowds who had gathered there for this spectacle saw what had taken place, they returned home, beating their breasts." This was the same crowd that had cried out, "Crucify, crucify him!" and that had sworn an oath in the words, "His blood be on us and on our children!"[8] But when they saw what happened, they beat their breasts and returned home. Was this perhaps because they had come only to feast their eyes on the drama of the Lord's death which had now come to an end? No! As the evangelists says: "They beat their breasts." From this and from other similar signs he had to have seen that there was still something else going on in their souls; something in the death of this particular righteous man had made them waver in their contempt or their hatred, so that they had become uncertain in themselves whether it had been of advantage to them to have brought about the death of the Prince of life. Now, it cannot be denied that with most of them this was only a passing impulse of the heart and mind. Nevertheless, some of these people were also certainly present afterwards on the days of Pentecost and heard Peter speak as he made public witness to the Prince of life. And indeed some from among these people, who were present for the second time beat their breasts although in a very different manner, and cried out: "Brothers, sisters, what should we do?"[9]

My good friends, may this day on which we annually celebrate the death of Christ in every congregation of Christians, in every nation where the name of Christ flourishes be such a blessed day! And certainly this is so, for among Christian peoples until the present time, there are those who have been implicated in the offense of the cross and are not ashamed to mock the Crucified One while simultaneously not disdaining outwardly to bear his name. These have not entirely died out. Indeed, one can say that some turn so completely away from him in their hearts and minds that they struggle in every way against being moved either by every significant sign that accompanied his life, or by the spirit and power that govern his words, or by the effects which his name has brought forth everywhere in the world. But also these, when they themselves see believers bow before the cross of the Redeemer in the devotion of their thankful hearts; when they hear how we renew the bond among ourselves to preach the blessings of his death until he comes; oh, in such an unpleasant attitude toward the

8. Eds.—Matt 27:25b.
9. Eds.—Acts 2:37.

Redeemer many hardened hearts will then become hesitant and beat their breast. And if there arises a fresh impulse of the Spirit and yet another, and the Word of the Lord knocks and beats ever more repeatedly at their ears and heart, oh then, they will also certainly turn away in the end from the way of corruption and become his and ours.

"But all his acquaintances, including the women who had followed him from Galilee, stood at a distance, watching all of these things." Standing close beneath his cross were only his mother and the disciple whom he had loved. As he had prophesied to them, the others had become scattered and only later were to be found with those who had been direct witnesses of his death. And those who were his relatives, his loyal women servants and women friends stood at a distance and beheld all of this. In a similar way, the influence of the Redeemer on earth began to have an effect on the heart and mind of his own mother, just as was the case when she had brought him to the temple and when she pondered all the words that he had spoken there. Similarly, his loyal female servants also now stood at a distance calmly contemplating the ebbing life of their dear Master and being edified by his departure to the Father inasmuch as in their innermost souls they appropriated everything that happened there.

But why did they stand at a distance? Oh my dear friends, this is a question we also might now ask of a large proportion of Christians! There are always really only comparatively few who associate with the cross of the Redeemer through thick and thin—those whom, like Mary and John, are brought from one another by Christ himself to the most inner and the most exact covenant of the heart. But let us not esteem too lightly those who stand more at a distance, but let us rather consider these women disciples of the Lord who also stood at a distance as a favorable sign. Many also who do not strive after a closer and to a certain extent personal relationship to Christ will certainly be deeply affected to their benefit in their inmost hearts and minds by the impression of his sacrificial death as by the calm greatness of his life. They will be now more, now less, now sooner, now later, consciously stimulated by this. Of those who also gathered less closely around the cross of the Redeemer we indeed know from all kinds of experiences that the contemplation of his death did not leave their hearts without a blessing. But certainly we will want to call out to these women disciples of the Lord: "Why do you stand at a distance? Come closer so that you will become more aware of how the glory of the only begotten Son is also revealed in the Crucified One. The more precisely you understand his last words in being closer to him, the more, if I may say so, you behold the look in his eyes as he departs, the more you are believing witnesses of his death, then the more you will be joyful witnesses of his resurrection, and in ways that are quicker, livelier, and more profound his whole being will sweep you away to eternal life. Indeed, there is still room here!"

All of those who are already aroused to faith, all who are already stirred by the glory of this day and by this vanishing of the darkness; by the light which has forever broken through and this tearing of the curtain; and by the blessings of the spiritual, sacred place which is now forever open to all—everyone can now gather ever more closely around the cross of him who departed on this day to return to heaven from the earth to which he had come for the salvation of human beings. His cross is the sign in which alone we can overcome all. Just as the Prince of our blessedness overcame all precisely on account of the fact that he was obedient to death, so we too are only able to overcome all when we take his cross upon ourselves and follow him. We are able to overcome as long as we are not afraid to enter the Reign of God, through the affliction that he has prepared for us, and as long as like him we are not afraid to be perfected through the cross and through suffering. Let us praise him anew for this faithfulness, and he will never cease to bless us from his cross on high. Amen.

Bibliography

Capetz, Paul E. "Friedrich Schleiermacher on the Old Testament." *Harvard Theological Review* 102 (2009) 297–325.

DeVries, Dawn. *Jesus Christ in the Preaching of Calvin and Schleiermacher.* Columbia Series in Reformed Theology. Louisville: Westminster John Knox, 1996.

Gesangbuch zum Gottesdienstlichen Gebrauch für evangelische Gemeinde: Mit Genehmigung. Eines hohen Ministerii der geistlichen Angelegenheiten. Berlin: Reimer, 1829.

Hirsch, Emanuel. *Schleiermachers Christusglaube: Drei Studien.* Gütersloh: Gütersloh/Mohn, 1968.

Jorgenson, Allen G. "Martin Luther on Preaching Christ Present." *International Journal of Systematic Theology* 16 (2014) 42–55.

Justin Martyr. "Dialogue with Trypho." Chapter 99. In *The Apostolic Fathers with Justin Martyr and Irenaeus.* Christian Classics Ethereal Library. https://ccel.org/ccel/justin_martyr/dialog_with_trypho/anf01.viii.iv.html.

Kelsey, Catherine L. *Schleiermacher's Preaching, Dogmatics, and Biblical Criticism: The Interpretation of Jesus Christ in the Gospel of John.* Princeton Theological Monograph Series 68. Eugene, OR: Pickwick Publications, 2007.

———. *Thinking about Christ with Schleiermacher.* Louisville: Westminster John Knox, 2003.

Luz, Ulrich. *Studies in Matthew.* Translated by Rosemary Selle. Grand Rapids: Eerdmans, 2005.

Redeker, Martin. *Schleiermacher: Life and Thought.* Translated by John Wallhausser. Philadelphia: Fortress, 1973.

Schleiermacher, Friedrich. *Christian Faith.* 2 vols. Translated by Terrence N. Tice et al. Edited by Catherine L. Kelsey and Terence N. Tice. Louisville: Westminster John Knox, 2016.

———. *Hermeneutics and Criticism and Other Writings.* Edited by Andrew Bowie. Translated by Andrew Bowie. Cambridge Texts in the History of Philosophy. Cambridge: Cambridge University Press, 1998.

———. *Kritische Gesamtausgabe III: Predigten.* 14 vols. Berlin: de Gruyter, 2011–2017.

———. *On the Doctrine of Election, with Special Reference to the Aphorisms of Dr Bretschneider.* Translated by Iain G. Nicol and Allen G. Jorgenson. Columbia Series in Reformed Theology. Louisville: Westminster John Knox, 2012.

———. *Sämmtliche Werke.* 30 vols. Berlin: Reimer, 1835–1884.

Smith, Robert H. *Matthew.* Augsburg Commentary on the New Testament. Minneapolis: Augsburg, 1989.

Sockness, Brent W. "The Forgotten Moralist: Friedrich Schleiermacher and the Science of Spirit." *Harvard Theological Review* 96 (2003) 317–48.

Streufert, Mary J. "Reclaiming Schleiermacher for Twenty-First-Century Atonement Theory: The Human and the Divine in Feminist Christology." *Feminist Theology* 15 (2006) 98–120.

Tice, Terrence N. *Schleiermacher.* Abingdon Pillars of Theology. Nashville: Abingdon, 2006.

———. *Schleiermacher: The Psychology of Christian Faith and Life.* Mapping the Tradition. Lanham, MD: Lexington Books/Fortress Academic, 2018.

———. *Schleiermacher's Sermons: A Chronological Listing and Account.* Schleiermacher Studies and Translations 15. Lewiston, NY: Mellen, 1997.

Verheyden, Jack C. "Introduction." In *The Life of Jesus,* by Friedrich Schleiermacher. Translated by S. MacLean Gilmour. 1975. Reprint, Lives of Jesus Series. Mifflintown, PA: Sigler, 1997.

Subject Index

anti-Semitism, 12–13
atonement
    classical theories of, x, 5–7
    and cross, 7, 15
    and preaching, 6
    and salvation of all, 4, 6

blessedness, 4, 4n15, 6–7, 29, 38–39, 48, 51, 104, 127–28

Christ, Jesus
    accepting help, 19, 69–70, 83–91
    calm in death, 67–68, 72, 76, 84, 111, 141
    as *Christus praesens*, 2–3
    and community, 2–8, 3n12, 16, 21, 23–24, 34, 107, 127, 129
    encountered in the sermon, 2–3
    as eternal image of the will of God, 123
    as example, 5, 18, 38, 42, 45, 47, 73, 79, 85, 93–94, 112
    as obedient to authorities and the law, 15, 44–48
    as preacher, 5, 11
    and redemption, 4–5, 8, 19–20, 82, 93–94, 96, 103, 119
    and suffering, 6–8, 13, 16–17, 19, 27–31, 40–61, 69–77, 79, 82–86, 91–92, 97, 123

church
    as body of Christ, 2
    as community, 2–3, 3n12
communion
    with Christ, 2–4, 68, 103–4, 130–31
    with fellow believers, 3–6, 8, 24, 89
    between God and the Redeemer, 17, 64–68, 94, 112, 125, 128–29
community of the Redeemer
    at the cross, 5–8, 16
    as locus of quickening activity, 24, 126–27
compassion, 6–7, 8, 70, 72–75
congregation, 3–4
covenant
    new, 15, 48, 113, 119, 130
    old, 15, 47–49, 97, 111, 119–20, 124, 136–38
creation
    as affirmed, 8–10, 12, 24
    and revelation, 125–26, 134–35
cross, 5–9, 14, 16, 19–20, 25, 31, 38, 58, 61, 77, 82–83, 94, 97, 99, 106, 115, 124, 140–42
    and crisis, 16
    as inspiration, 38
    not precondition for forgiveness, 5–8, 14
    as revelation of divine love, 38–39
    as a scandal and foolishness, 38, 100

SUBJECT INDEX

cross *(continued)*
    as symbol/cipher, 25
    as turning point in history, 7, 9–10, 24, 59, 84, 104, 119
crucifixion, 14, 24, 123, 127

damnation, 13n61
death
    of believers with Christ, 15, 125–28, 136
    and the glory of the Redeemer, 31–39, 128
    of Jesus
        as end of sacrifice, 22–23, 118–32
        as reconciling, 83, 104, 114
        as sacrificial, 38, 119, 130, 141
        and signs accompanying it, 134–38
        as turning point, 7, 21, 24, 59, 84, 104, 119, 136
    Jesus' experience of in comparison with ours, 22, 66–68, 112
    a moment of living, 22, 110–12, 116
    as an opening of reality, 21–22
    as ordered by eternal decree, 22, 27, 47–48, 100
decree, divine
    bridging spiritual and material, 9, 24, 101
    as goal of the Redeemer, 57, 59, 71, 102
    and necessity, 13, 27–28, 40, 99
    and the new covenant, 47–49
    now disclosed, 31, 123
    orders death, 11, 22, 26, 28, 38, 47–48, 99–100
    single in nature, 4–7, 13, 137
    and universalism, 21, 59–60, 136
    at work in our activity, 20, 101
despair, 17, 64, 67, 69–70, 106
destiny, 38, 48, 56–57, 59, 68, 85, 97, 100, 135
disunity, 89
divisiveness, 89
doubt, doubtful, 29, 55, 106, 139

election, 6, 9, 13
enmity, 19, 38, 67, 88, 90, 93–94, 129–31
equanimity, 25, 68, 112
eternal
    life, 10, 33, 50, 116–17, 142
    and temporal, 14, 22, 30, 33, 59, 67, 70, 109–110, 117, 138
    as transfiguring the earthly, 9–10
experience, 5, 9–13, 17, 22, 33, 48, 51, 56, 70, 74, 78, 80, 88, 91, 107, 116, 118, 135

faith, 3, 3n10, 14–15, 17, 24, 30–34, 30n5, 36–37, 48, 59–60, 65, 70, 91–96, 103–4, 125–26, 128, 136–39
    active in love, 104
    caused by Holy Spirit through the Word, 37
    in contrast to works, 48
    and doubt, 139
    and proclamation, 23, 30–31
    present in disciples before the crucifixion, 32–34
    and union with the Redeemer, 3, 15, 30n5, 103–4, 125–26
feeling, 5–6, 5n21, 32, 37, 39, 55, 64–65, 73–74, 89, 94, 104, 116, 118, 121, 134
forgive, forgiveness, 14, 19, 22–23, 29–32, 34, 36, 38, 59, 63, 76, 87, 93, 114–16
free, freedom, 4, 10, 15, 46, 48–50, 56, 59, 73–74, 84, 86, 94, 127, 131, 135
friendship, 75
fulfil, fulfilment, 17n66, 20–21, 27–30, 42, 84, 86, 89, 97–102, 104–5, 138

glory of the Redeemer
    and God-consciousness, 13–14, 29
    illumining suffering, 13, 28, 71, 73
    and proclamation, 14, 29–32
God-consciousness
    and community, 2–6, 16
    demonstrative of piety, 5
    and glory, 13–14, 29
    uninterrupted in the Redeemer, 16–17, 22, 64–65
goodness, as not entirely vanished in humans, 93

SUBJECT INDEX

good, the, 19, 93–94, 126
gospel, 5n22, 10n50, 25, 137–38
grace, 4, 8–9, 60, 103, 114–15, 134, 137–38

history, 7–8, 10, 10n50, 18, 21, 24, 72, 136, 138
human nature, 4, 9, 25, 91–93, 106, 109, 125, 135–36
hymns, 78, 119

image of God, 21, 50, 64, 106, 123, 126, 137–38
Israel, 15, 33, 44, 55, 69, 71–72, 75

joy, 18, 53, 64, 68, 74–75, 85, 93, 98, 105, 107, 111, 122, 128
Judaism, 12, 12n58, 23n79
judge, judgment, 43, 73, 92, 122
justification, 4, 20, 32, 96, 122

law, divine, 15, 42–50, 87, 90, 113, 135
love, divine, 9, 23, 28, 38–39, 57, 60, 74, 92, 117, 126

merit, 84, 101–2, 105, 122

obedience, 7, 14–15, 24, 41–42, 44–48, 52, 81, 84, 117, 123, 130–31, 137
omnipotence, 21, 110

pain, 55–56, 67, 69–70, 73, 75, 82, 84–85, 87, 90, 97, 126, 134
participation in Jesus, 8, 15, 23, 58, 75
passion, 2, 8, 11, 15–16, 19
peace, 17, 22, 54, 54n5, 61, 68, 71, 88, 98, 105–6, 114–15, 132, 135, 138–39
piety, 5, 8, 21, 78
power
   of evil, 14, 61
   of the gospel, 4, 25, 78–79, 137–38
   of the law, 15, 43–44, 48
   of love, 76, 92, 115
   of the Redeemer, 4, 23, 30, 50–51, 63, 77, 82–83, 89, 100, 126
   of the Redeemer's death, 82–83, 120, 122, 128
   of sin, 124–25, 127, 130
prayer, high priestly, 21, 102
preaching
   and Reign of God, 14, 139
   and Schleiermacher's identity, 1–2
priest, priesthood, 25, 43, 57, 90, 119, 122, 133, 137–39
pride, 87
proclamation, 2, 14, 30–31, 34, 139
prophecy, 27–28, 86
providence, 59, 100
psalms, 18, 69, 110

redemption, 4–5, 8, 11–12, 14, 17, 19–21, 65, 82, 89, 93–94, 96, 119
   and Christ's death, 5, 119
   continued in the community of the Redeemer, 4–5, 8
   and justification, 20, 96
   and proclamation, 4, 11, 14
   and suffering, 8, 19, 82
   as universal, 12, 21, 89
repentance, 29–32, 34, 36
resurrection, 5, 7, 14, 24, 27, 29, 34, 40, 51, 98, 128, 140, 142
ruler of this world, 40–41, 43–44, 48–49, 59

sacrifice, 6, 22–23, 119–24, 128, 130–32
salvation, 3–6, 8, 13n61, 16, 18, 21, 39, 57–61, 71, 83, 85, 89, 96, 115, 118–19, 123, 137, 142
sanctified, sanctification, 17, 58, 61, 68, 78, 103, 105, 119, 130–32
Savior, 21, 125
scattered, 15, 53–55, 61, 141
Scripture
   as comfort, 78–79
   Hebrew, as inferior, 18, 78–79
sermon
   content of, 2–3, 10–11
   and last seven words of Christ, 5
sign, 39, 86, 98, 112, 133–36, 138–40, 142
sin
   of commission, 15, 124
   external to the redeemed, 24, 127–29
   guilt of taken away, 130–31

sin *(continued)*
    memorials of, 22, 120–24
    of omission, 15
    as systemic, 23
    universal in scope, 15, 23, 121, 123

Spirit, Holy
    as Advocate sent to disciples, 36–37, 49–50, 96, 104
    bears witness to our faith, 77
    connection between Spirit and nature, 9, 24, 134
    enlightens Scripture's reading, 103
    and innate revelation of God, 136
    inspires throughout history, 18, 77–78
    works with Word, 126, 141

suffer, suffering, 6–8, 13, 16–17, 19, 27–30, 42, 47, 54–61, 65–66, 69–77, 82–88, 97, 99–100, 123, 128
    of the believer, 8, 16–17, 73, 76, 99–100
    that is dignified, 70, 84
    and glory, 13, 13n61, 28–30, 96, 128
    and loneliness, 16, 54–55, 57–58, 60–61
    and necessity, 27, 34–35, 42
    and obedience, 46–48
    physical, 19, 70, 74, 82, 85, 97
    purification of, 73
    separates and scatters, 55
    and sympathy for others, 16–17, 56, 70, 73–75

teaching, 25, 33, 43, 50, 80, 84

universalism, 4, 6, 12, 13n61, 25, 89

victory, 58, 61, 83, 91, 94, 98–99, 131, 136

will, divine, 6, 21, 24, 29, 42, 84, 89, 103, 114, 123, 127, 129, 131, 137
witness, 18, 71, 74, 77–79, 92, 99, 103, 106, 140–42
Word, divine, 23–24, 37, 69, 80, 106, 109, 126
works, human 84–85, 124, 131

Name Index

Aquinas, Thomas, 2

Brondos, David A., x

Calvin, John, 1

Capetz, Paul E., 12n58

DeVries, Dawn, 1–2, 1n1, 2n4, 2n6, 2n8, 5n22, 11, 11n51, 11n54

Hirsch, Emmanuel, 5n23, 7, 7nn33–34, 8, 8nn39–40, 9, 9n44, 10, 10nn45–50, 13, 13n59

Jorgenson, Allen G., ix–x, 2n8, 25

Kelsey, Catherine L., 2n4, 2n7

Lawler, Edwina, x

Luther, Martin, 2, 2n8, 15

Luz, Ulrich, 17n66

Martyr, Justin, 17n66

Nicol, Iain G., ix–x, 25

Redeker, Martin, 1n3, 2, 2n9, 3n11, 9, 9n41

Smith, Robert H., 17n66

Sockness, Brent W., 2n4

Streufert, Mary J., 2, 2n7, 3n10, 4, 4n17, 5n20

Tice, Terrence N., x, 1, 1n2, 4n14, 6n24, 6n26, 11, 11n53, 12n55, 12n57, 25, 26n1

Verheyden, Jack C., 14, 14nn62–63

Scripture Index

Genesis

9:12a	135n2
9:15b	135n2

Leviticus

16:15–19	23n78

Joshua

1:5	64n6

1 Kings

19:9–14	37n23

Psalms

19:1–4	101n11
22	65–66, 69
22:1	17, 98n6, 111n3
22:3	69n12
22:4–5a	72n17
22:15	85n5
22:16	19
22:18	77n26
22:22	72n20
22:27	72n21
31:5	111n4
31:6	111n3
40:7b	86n6
40:8	86n6
148:13	30n4

Isaiah

42:3	98n5
53:12	35n15
58:6–11	23n79
63:16	30n4

Matthew

5:17	45n13
8:20b	84n4
10:24a	136n3
11:28	132n21
12:20	98n5
15:24	44n10
16:16	33n9
16:17	33n10

SCRIPTURE INDEX

Matthew *(continued)*

18:20	58n10
20:16	102n15
25:24	107n23
26:39	41n3
27:25b	140n8
27:46	17, 17n66, 63, 98n6
27:50	108n2
28:19	47n18

Mark

4:26	37n20
15:1–2	139n7
15:37	108n2
15:39b	139n6

Luke

2:29–32	71n15
2:29–30	71n15
3:22b	60n17
4:30	42n7
12:49	36n17
22:42	42n4
23:28b	55n8
23:34a	59n15, 87n7
23:43	9
23:43a	19
23:43b	63n2
23:44–49	24, 133
23:45	8–9
23:46	21, 64n5, 108
24:21a	33n12
24:25–26	33n11, 40n2
24:25	13–14, 26
24:26	13, 26
24:46	29n2
24:47	29n2, 30n3

John

1:5	57n9
1:14b	60n16
1:16	117n11
1:29	128n12
1:46	122n4
3:15	116n8
3:29–32	72n16
3:30	20n73
4	18
4:24	74n23
5:19	59n13
5:20	59n13
6:63	34n13
7	18
7:30	43n9
7:37	81n2
8:6a	45n14
8:20	43n9
8:56	71n14
9:5	31n6
10:30	58n11
10:31	42n6
11:50	122n5
12:24	36n19
12:32	39n25, 113n7
14:2	67n7
14:6a	113n5
14:6b	113n6
14:9	58n12
14:9b	137n5
14:30–31	14, 40
14:30	43n8, 45n16, 49n22
14:31	46n17, 49n22, 51n23
16:7	36n18
16:12	104n19
16:16	67n9
16:28	53n2, 67n8
16:30	54n3
16:32	15, 53
16:32b	64n3
16:33	54n5
16:33a	54n4
17	21, 100n10
17:4	71n13
17:6	71n13
17:8	102n14

SCRIPTURE INDEX

17:16	102n14
17:24a	60n18
18:8b	55n6
19:28–29	18, 81
19:28	95n2
19:28a	95n3
19:30	59n14, 72n19
19:30a	20, 95
19:30b	64n4
20:30	36n16
21:22	51n24

Acts of the Apostles

2:3	32n8
2:37	140n9
4:12	30n4, 39n26
26:18	31n6

Romans

1:18	136n4
1:25	126n10
2:19	31n6
3:20	122n2
3:23	103n16
4:25	20, 32n7, 96n4
5:8	131n20
5:10	83n3
6:4	125n8
7:24–25	131n17
7:24	131n18
7:25	131n18
8:1–8	129n14
8:1	131n16, 131n18
8:18	76n25
8:26	77
8:28	21n76, 107n25
8:28a	62n19
8:30	107n24
11:33	37n21
12:1	131n19
12:15b	55n7
16:25	48n19

1 Corinthians

1:23	38n24
1:30	62n20, 103n17, 117n10
5:57	131n18
12:7	105n21
15:28	3n10, 21n74
15:50a	99n8

2 Corinthians

5:16a	100n9
5:17	130n15
5:19a	102n13

Galatians

2:19	48n20
2:20	30n5, 48n20, 125n9
3:13	48n21
3:14	48n21
4:4	44n12
5:22	105n22

Ephesians

1:21	30n4
2:10	21n75
2:14	103n18

Philippians

1:9	30n4
2:6–7	101n12
3:12	127n11
3:13b	68n10
4:4	73n22

Colossians

1:15b	51n25
1:26	48n19
1:27	48n19

1 Thessalonians

4:3	68n11

Hebrews

3:6	45n15
10:5–7	128n13
10:8–12	22, 119
10:10b	123n6
10:16	129
10:22	125n7
12:2a	105n20, 117n9
12:9–10	39n28
13:8	35n14

1 Peter

2:24	98n7

1 John

2:16	122n3
4:8	74n24

www.ingramcontent.com/pod-product-compliance
Lightning Source LLC
Chambersburg PA
CBHW022121160426
43197CB00009B/1103